Unborn Children of America

and

Other Family Procedures

Six Plays

Michele Markarian

Fomite
Burlington, VT

Copyright 2015 © by Michele Markarian

All rights reserved. No part of this book may be reproduced in any form or by any means without the prior written consent of the publisher, except in the case of brief quotations used in reviews and certain other noncommercial uses permitted by copyright law.

Please contact the author at michele.markarian@gmail.com for permission for professional or amateur production, public readings or any other performance of these plays.

This is a work of fiction. Names, characters, places and incidents are either the product of the author's imagination or are used fictitiously. Any resemblance to actual persons, living or dead, events or locales is entirely coincidental.

ISBN-13: 978-1-942515-09-8
Library of Congress Control Number: 2015938866

Fomite
58 Peru Street
Burlington, VT 05401
www.fomitepress.com

Front cover image - *Breakaway* © by Hannah Goodwin
Back cover photo -

In memory of Sue Tashjian

Acknowledgements

To Donna and Marc at Fomite Press, for believing in the project
To Hannah Goodwin, for the gorgeous cover art
To fellow scribes Jean Klingler and Joel Wachman for their honesty and enthusiasm
To Steve Markarian, who conceived of the dedoption agency at a family dinner
To those willing and talented participants who sat around my dining room table and brought the words to life: Matthew Bernstein, Cristi Catt, Amy Ford, Dan Ford, Eliza Gagnon, Jim Loutzenheiser, Mary McCarthy, Jayne Ogata, Michael O'Halloran, Eric Ronis and Jason Taylor.

Contents

Unborn Children of America	1
Parents of Typical Children	73
The Octomom Conceives	95
The Dedoption	115
Whose Bag Is It, Anyway?	195
The Real Family	215

Unborn Children of America

Unborn Children of America
Cast of Characters

DINA — A 41 year old graphic designer, attractive. She has been trying to conceive a baby, and is married to JACK.

JACK — A 42 year old self-employed electrician, boyish in appearance. He is married to DINA.

LIZ — DINA's best friend from high school, 41 years old. She is attractive and overweight, and has just taken a new job.

SCOTT — 35-40 year old husband of LIZ who works in his father's business.

Scene

DINA and JACK's home, just outside of the city

Time

The not-too-distant future

Scene 1

Setting: We are in the living room of DINA and JACK. There is a sofa, a loveseat, and a coffee table bearing a bottle of wine, some glasses, and two bowls, one with guacamole, one with chips.

At Rise: It is four in the afternoon. DINA and JACK are awaiting their guests, LIZ and SCOTT. DINA runs around nervously, straightening out the room. JACK sits on the couch, reading a magazine. The doorbell rings.

DINA
Shoot, that's them.

JACK
(Looks at watch)
What the heck, Deen? They're early.

DINA
(Runs around straightening up the room)
Just a minute! Help me, with you?

JACK
What for? He's just gonna wanna go outside and shoot hoops.

(Doorbell rings again)

DINA
Coming! Don't be so negative, okay?

JACK
I'm not being negative, I'm just stating a fact.

DINA
This is my best friend's husband we're talking about.
    (Opens door)
Hi!
    (LIZ and SCOTT walk in)

LIZ
Hey!
    (Gives DINA a big hug)
Jack!
    (Hugs Jack, tentatively)

JACK
Hey, Liz. Scott.

SCOTT
Hey, man!
    (Gives JACK a hug. Embraces DINA, a little too enthusiastically)

JACK
Hey, uh, that's enough. Uh, just kidding.

SCOTT
Didn't peg you as the jealous type!
    (Still hugging DINA)

DINA

No. He's not.

LIZ

Well, I am! Hands off!
    (LIZ swats at SCOTT. They all laugh)

DINA

Come in! Have a seat.

SCOTT

Dude, you still have that basketball hoop?

JACK

'Course.

SCOTT

Would you mind — it was a long car ride.

LIZ

Well…

JACK

Was just telling Dina how I hoped you'd wanna play hoops.

LIZ

Go ahead, hon. Dina and I can catch up.

JACK

Beer?

SCOTT

Oh, yeah. For you —
    (SCOTT holds out a brown paper bag)

JACK

You want one?

SCOTT

Are you kidding me?
    (SCOTT and JACK exit stage left)

DINA

You look great!

LIZ

No. Well, I lost five pounds.

DINA

You can tell.

LIZ

I feel like you can tell. My clothes don't feel as tight.

DINA

No, really. You can tell.

LIZ

Thanks. Forty more to go. Well, maybe thirty.
    (LIZ sees some guacamole on the coffee table)
Guac?

DINA

Yeah. Please. Help yourself. Hey, you want some wine?

LIZ

I shouldn't, but —

DINA

Come on.

LIZ

Okay. Why not?
(LIZ moves to the couch and helps herself to some dip)

DINA

(Uncorking wine)
So what's been going on? You changed jobs?

LIZ

(Tries to speak, but mouth is full of dip. Swallows)
Yup. Six — no, seven months ago.

DINA

How's it going?

LIZ

Dina, I didn't realize how burnt out I was until I made the change.

DINA

You were there a long time.

LIZ

Seventeen years! Crazy!

DINA

Oh my God, that's so crazy. Although I should talk — I've been at my job, what? Thirteen? No, wait. Maybe — what year is it?

LIZ

Dina, it was the best thing I ever did.

DINA

Two thousand seven, two thousand eight — two thousand-fifteen years. God, that's so sick.

LIZ

Anyway, enough about work. How are things with Jack? Is his job stable right now?

DINA

Oh, yeah. That whole rough patch — employed, unemployed, self-employed — totally — you know. We worked through it. He's fine. He's making — decent money.

LIZ

Oh, good.

DINA

Yeah. No, it's all good. And Scott?

LIZ

Scott. Scott's just lucky. You know that. Who knows where he'd be if his dad didn't have that company? Not that he doesn't contribute —

DINA

No, I'm sure —

LIZ

So things are stable. That's good.

DINA

Yeah. Yeah. I was worried for awhile, but things are good.

LIZ

Good.

DINA
(Takes a chip and puts it in the guacamole)

LIZ
Any news?

DINA
What kind of news?

LIZ
You know. News.

DINA
Uh — let me think. Um — oh, you know that logo I spent six months on?

LIZ
Logo?

DINA
Finally approved. My God, I thought we were never going to get off the ground with that one! My boss was like —

LIZ
That's not news.

DINA
What kind of news?

LIZ
You know.
    (Pause)
Dina! You uh, you trying?

DINA
(Holds up a finger, swallows chip)
Trying —

LIZ
You know. Kids.

DINA
Oh. That. Well — why? Are you?

LIZ
Why do you think I'm trying to lose weight? I can't get pregnant like this.

DINA
People do it.

LIZ
Yeah, well, not me. I'll never get the weight off. Afterwards, I mean.

DINA
I guess. We're getting up there, Liz. It might be time.

LIZ
Does this mean you're trying?

DINA
Well, we've stopped — you know. We don't use anything. We figure we'll leave it up to chance. If it's meant to be, it's meant to be.

LIZ
Really?

DINA
Yeah. It's kind of exciting. Adds an element of danger to the whole thing.

LIZ
Huh. I guess I'll be there soon enough.

DINA
Maybe we'll have our kids together. Wouldn't that be great?

LIZ
How long have you been trying?

DINA
We're not exactly trying. We're just not using anything.

LIZ
So how long?

DINA
Mmmmm……I don't know. Maybe a year and a half?

LIZ
A year and a half?

DINA
Yeah. That sounds right.

LIZ
And nothing's happened?

DINA
Well, it's not as if we're trying….I mean, really trying.

LIZ
You're having unprotected sex!

DINA
I know.

LIZ
Are you using an ovulation kit?

DINA
Are you kidding me? Jack would kill me.

LIZ
(Waits expectantly)

DINA
Of course I am.

LIZ
And nothing's happened?

DINA
Nope.

LIZ
Shoot.

DINA
I know.

LIZ
Has Jack been tested?

DINA

He doesn't want it badly enough to be tested. You know Jack. If it doesn't happen, it doesn't happen. He's fine either way.

LIZ

And it's not you —

DINA

We know it's not me.
    (Pause)
Anyway. So your job.

LIZ

My job.
    (Looks at DINA thoughtfully)
It's a non-profit, and after years of raping and pillaging people, I am so happy to be doing something good for a change.

DINA

That's awesome. And so not like you.

LIZ

    (Hits Dina playfully)

DINA

Although you always did like to help people.

LIZ

This place is great, Dina.

DINA

What exactly are you doing?

LIZ

Well, my official title is Specimen Placement Specialist. It's mostly outreach, trying to find homes for what will be beautiful, brainy babies.

DINA

Really. Wow. What's the name of the company?

LIZ

The Unborn Children of America.

DINA

I never heard of it.

LIZ

It's a fairly new company, which is why there's so much room for growth. It's really only two years old.

DINA

Oh, wow. So you have a chance here to carve out a decent niche for yourself.

LIZ

Yeah, but that's not why I'm doing it. I feel really strongly about the company's mission and making it happen.

DINA

This is so not like you.

LIZ

Maybe I just hadn't found myself.

DINA

Maybe.
    (DINA takes a chip)
What is the company's mission?

LIZ

It's hard to explain.

DINA

The Unborn Children of America.

LIZ

Well, they're not necessarily of America, although they originated here. They can be shipped anywhere. We have had a few emigrate to Canada, The United Kingdom, even Israel.

DINA

Really? How is that even possible?

LIZ

Oh, that part's easy. We just wrap them up in the appropriate storage containers and ship them.

DINA

How do you do that if they haven't been born?

LIZ

This is the great part.

DINA

Okay.

LIZ

Oh, gosh — how do I explain this?

DINA
(Smiles and shrugs)

LIZ
This man — let's call him Mr. X — has a PhD in Biophysics. He's six feet tall, weighs 175 pounds, and has no genetic history of alcohol, drug abuse or mental illness.

DINA
Okay —

LIZ
Mr. X really wants to pass his genes onto the next generation, but hasn't found the right woman.

DINA
You're kidding me.

LIZ
I know. Hard to believe, but it's true.

DINA
Wow.

LIZ
I know. Crazy. Back to Mr. X. He just hasn't found the right woman. Of course, if you're Mr. X, you're bound to be picky. You can't marry just anyone, right?

DINA
I guess — yeah, you're right. Although I've seen it happen. Remember Cy?

LIZ
Oh my God. Cy. From high school?

DINA
Yes! He was — gorgeous.

LIZ
Was he Princeton?

DINA
Yes. Princeton. Went on to become some kind of physicist —

LIZ
And he married that schlub —

DINA
I know. What was her name?

LIZ
Umm…oh God, it's on the tip of my tongue. Sandy?

DINA
Nancy!

LIZ
Nancy!

DINA
What a slouch.

LIZ
I never got it.

DINA
Had to be low self-esteem.

LIZ

Well, Mr. X does not have this problem. He has self-esteem. He can't just settle.

DINA

He's not conceited, is he?

LIZ

(Horrified)
No! He has enough self-esteem to recognize a Nancy when he sees one, and to run in the opposite direction!

DINA

Oh. Okay.

LIZ

So four years ago, Mr. X decides to donate some sperm to a sperm bank. You know what that is?

DINA

I'm familiar with sperm banks. Duh.

LIZ

Sorry. You'd be surprised how many people aren't.

DINA

No!

LIZ

Yeah. A lot of outreach is education.

DINA

So Mr. X —

LIZ

Right. Mr. X donates his superior sperm to a sperm bank and unfortunately, no one wants it.

DINA

Why not? What is wrong with people?

LIZ

No kidding! Mr. X is a total catch, right? He's got a PhD from an Ivy League school! His genetics are peerless! He's tall! Yet because of a surplus of sperm, his future progeny may not make it in this lifetime.

DINA

Does he have poor social skills?

LIZ

What?

DINA

Does he have poor social skills? A lot of these uber brainy men are just — asocial, you know?

LIZ

Mr. X is definitely not asocial.

DINA

Then I don't understand. I thought that everyone wanted sperm like Mr. X's.

LIZ

Well, they did, but apparently the market overestimated the trend to have babies with sperm donors. Poor Mr. X's specimen is just sitting in a freezer, wasting away.

                    DINA
God, that's terrible.

                    LIZ
This is where I come in.

                    DINA
Oh my God. Liz — are you?

                    LIZ
What?

                    DINA
You know —

                    LIZ
Dina —

                    DINA
Are you — shooting up with Mr. X?

                    LIZ
No! I told you, I can't. Too much weight on.

                    DINA
Would Scott even allow it?

                    LIZ
He wouldn't have to know. But — it's out of the question. At least for another thirty pounds.

                    DINA
Oh.

                    LIZ
But — what I do is take people like Mr. X and match them up with appropriate families.

                    DINA
Really?

                    LIZ
Yeah.

                    DINA
How do you find the families?

                    LIZ
Well, some of them contact us directly. Others we find through fertility clinics, adoption lists — we also advertise. Uh, parents' blogs, the Purple Pages —

                    DINA
The gay and lesbian directory?

                    LIZ
Exactly.

                    DINA
What kind of people are looking for Mr. X?

                    LIZ
People who want kids, but either can't afford adoption or a sperm donor.

                    DINA
How do they afford you?

LIZ
They don't. It's non-profit. Pay what you can. Sliding scale.

DINA
How do you make money?

LIZ
The sperm banks, Deen. They are overflowing with unwanted sperm. They pay us to find a home for it. And thank God they do. Otherwise, Mr. X's genes would die out.

DINA
Huh.

LIZ
This is what I mean. How can I not feel good about what I do for a living?

DINA
No, it sounds great.
    (DINA takes a swig of wine)
So, have you seen anyone from high school?

LIZ
Dina, can I do you a favor?

DINA
What kind of favor?

LIZ
A good favor.

DINA
What kind of favor?
>(DINA holds out her glass to be refilled. LIZ pours her more wine)

LIZ
Can I give you Mr. X's sperm?

DINA
>(Sputters on wine)

WHAT?

LIZ
Seriously. Let me give you Mr. X's sperm.

DINA
Liz, I can't take Mr. X's sperm.

LIZ
Why not?

DINA
Come on, Liz. What would Jack say?

LIZ
He wouldn't have to know.

DINA
But I want Jack's baby! We're married.

LIZ
A year and a half, Dina? What the heck?

DINA
Maybe I'm just stressed.

LIZ
That's bullshit and you know it. Has Jack been tested?

DINA
I told you. No.

LIZ
Mr. X has.

DINA
I don't want to hear about Mr. X anymore. I'm done with Mr. X.

LIZ
Okay.

DINA
I can't believe you.
    (Pause)
So how's your sister doing? I haven't seen her since — God, when was I at your family's last? Six years ago?

LIZ
Do you want to see a picture?

DINA
Of your sister?

LIZ
Of Mr. X.

DINA

No!
    (DINA stands up and goes to get another bottle of wine.
    LIZ has a chip. DINA returns)
You have a picture?

LIZ

Uh huh.

DINA

I suppose it wouldn't hurt to see a picture.

LIZ
    (Pulls a photo out of her purse. Puts it in front of DINA)

DINA
    (Picks up photo. Stares)
For real?

LIZ

Yup.

DINA

Wow.

LIZ

No kidding, right?

DINA

I mean —

LIZ

I know.

DINA

He is something.

LIZ

Yeah.

DINA

And nobody wants his sperm?

LIZ

People are stupid, Dina. People are so stupid.

DINA

Why can't he meet the right girl?

LIZ

I told you. With his pedigree and high degree of confidence, he can't be sure he *will* meet the right girl.

DINA

Huh.

    (DINA refills her wine)

LIZ

Oh, talk about a nightmare — do you know who I ran into?

DINA

Huh? No.

LIZ

Penny.

DINA

Penny. Penny Ventropolis?

LIZ
Yup.

DINA
God. Where did you run into her?

LIZ
(Refills wine)
I probably shouldn't say.

DINA
Liz!

LIZ
It's confidential.

DINA
Since when were you and Penny Ventropolis ever close? You used to call her Henny Penny. Now all of a sudden it's confidential?

LIZ
Okay. Whatever. I shouldn't have said anything.

DINA
Liz!

LIZ
What?

DINA
You just can't come out with oh, that nightmare Henny Penny and then not tell me! That's not fair.

LIZ
Okay, fine. But if you say one word, you are dead meat, you hear me?

DINA
Fine. I won't say a word.

LIZ
Promise?

DINA
Yes.

LIZ
I mean it.

DINA
So do I.

LIZ
She's one of my clients.

DINA
Henny Penny?

LIZ
Penny.

DINA
Oh. Sorry. Penny.
    (DINA is getting a little drunk)

LIZ
She and her husband came to me five or six months ago and — it was sad.

DINA

Henny Penny's married?

LIZ

He's a really nice guy.

DINA

Wow. I'm surprised.

LIZ

But —

DINA

But?

LIZ

His sperm is a no-go.

DINA

What do you mean?

LIZ

You better not tell anybody. I could get into so much trouble.

DINA

I won't! I promise.

LIZ

His sperm has no — oomph.

DINA

Oomph?

LIZ

Mobility.

DINA

Oh. What does that mean?

LIZ

It means that if Penny wants to get pregnant, her husband isn't going to be the one to do it.

DINA

How do you know?

LIZ

I am so breaking client confidentiality here.
    (LIZ pours herself some more wine)

DINA

Liz, you know I am good for it.

LIZ

Dina, it was awful. She looked awful. First of all, they'd been trying for nearly two years.
    (Looks at DINA meaningfully)

DINA

So? Some people take longer.

LIZ

Then they tried IVF for another three years. Do you know how expensive IVF is?

DINA

    (Shakes head)

LIZ
Let's just say that by the time they contacted the Unborn Children of America, they were in the hole about 120 grand.

DINA
Are you serious?

LIZ
Absolutely. Don't you dare —

DINA
I won't! My God, how many times do I have to —

LIZ
And it had taken its toll, let me tell you. She was a wreck.

DINA
Well, she was never really —

LIZ
She looks great now, though.

DINA
-a looker. Why? What's so great about now?

LIZ
She's three months pregnant.

DINA
Oh. How did that happen?

LIZ
What have I been telling you?

DINA
Mr. X? Is she pregnant with Mr. X's baby?

LIZ
No. Not Mr. X. Another guy.

DINA
How come she didn't want Mr. X?

LIZ
Well, Mr. X is dark.

DINA
I know. He's so beautiful.
        (DINA picks up photo and strokes it)

LIZ
Penny's husband is blonde. Even though it wouldn't be his sperm, he wanted the baby to look like him.

DINA
You can do that?

LIZ
Yeah.

DINA
Jack has brown hair. Brownish black.

LIZ
I know.

DINA
Did Penny want Mr. X?

LIZ
He wasn't an option for Penny, Dina. She needed a blonde.

DINA
Did you show her Mr. X?

LIZ
No. I wouldn't do that. It wouldn't be fair.

DINA
To Mr. X?

LIZ
To Penny.

DINA
Why Penny? Why not Mr. X?

LIZ
If you know that somebody needs a blonde, why taunt them with a Mr. X?

DINA
I get it. So Liz, you think that Mr. X was a better catch than the guy Penny picked?

LIZ
Dina!

DINA
I'm just asking!

LIZ
This is SO unethical. I'm not going there.

                            DINA
Well, if you could pick between Mr. X and Penny's blonde baby-daddy, who would you pick?

                            LIZ
Stop.

                            DINA
No! I'm just asking.

                            LIZ
This is really inappropriate.

                            DINA
You'd pick Mr. X.

                            LIZ
Dina!

                            DINA
Admit it. You love him.

                            LIZ
As a professional, I refuse to talk about this.

                            DINA
You do. You love him.

                            LIZ
The point is, Penny made the right choice for her. And they're thrilled. I don't think they ever thought they'd see the day.

DINA
(Teary)
Really?

LIZ
Yeah.

DINA
That's so beautiful, Liz.

LIZ
I know.

DINA
You're right — that is some amazing work you're doing with the Unopened Children of America.

LIZ
Unborn.

DINA
Unborn.

LIZ
I know. It really makes people happy. I help make people happy.

DINA
That's so awesome. I wish I could do that.

LIZ
You can.

DINA
No, I don't think so.

LIZ
Mr. X would like nothing more than to leave a legacy. Of himself.

DINA
I can't. Maybe in a few years.

LIZ
How many years do you think you have, Dina?

DINA
You are such a bitch —

LIZ
Come on! I'm in the same boat! Why do you think I'm dieting? If I were you, I'd jump on this!

DINA
What if I get pregnant?

LIZ
Isn't that the point?
    (DINA is silent)

LIZ
Don't you want to get pregnant?

DINA
Yes, I want to get pregnant! Of course I want to get pregnant!

LIZ
Okay —

DINA
I mean, I am SO ready to have a baby!

LIZ

Right —

DINA

And Jack? Jack could care less.

LIZ

Do you really think?

DINA

Please. He'd be perfectly happy if we stayed like this, just the two of us, living in our own little teenaged bubble. My God, he wouldn't even have health insurance if it weren't for me. Not that he'd notice.

LIZ

I wonder if they're not all like that. I swear, Scott keeps trying to feed me so that I'll stay fat.

DINA

So yeah, to answer your question, I want a baby. With or without Jack.

LIZ

Then you should have one.

DINA

I know.

LIZ

Now you know how Mr. X feels.

DINA

Poor guy. I totally get it.

LIZ

It's what you do if you haven't met the right woman.

DINA

I guess so.
    (Pause)
Sometimes I wonder if I'm doing the right thing.

LIZ

With Jack?

DINA

No. With my job.

LIZ

    (Shrugs)
It's a job. You've been there forever.

DINA

Yeah, I know. But who am I helping? When I think of Henny Penny and her husband —

LIZ

I know. I still can't believe my luck.

DINA

I'll do it.

LIZ

What?

DINA

I'll do it. I'll take Mr. X's sperm.

LIZ

Oh my God. Dina.
> (LIZ jumps up and takes Dina's hands)

What about Jack? What are you gonna tell him?

DINA

I don't know. I'll figure it out. This is my chance to do something important.

LIZ

Yes, it is! Dina —
> (LIZ gets teary)

If I have no other purpose than to get you and Mr. X's sperm together, I will be fulfilled.

DINA

Oh, Liz.
> (The two embrace)

So, do you have it? Mr. X's sperm?

LIZ

Dina, it'll be shipped to you within 24 hours.

DINA

Really?

LIZ

I promise.

DINA

Then what?

LIZ

He'll come with instructions.

JACK
(Offstage)
Hey, Dina, you want me to start the grill?

DINA
Don't tell Jack!

LIZ
Don't worry.

DINA
Sure.
(To LIZ)
How much do I owe you?

LIZ
I told you — it's free.

DINA
Really?

LIZ
Really.

DINA
Oh, my God, Liz. I'm going to have a baby.

LIZ
I know.

DINA
(Indicates picture)
Can I keep this? To show him? Or her?

LIZ
Of course you can.

DINA
Liz, thank you.
    (LIZ and DINA embrace)

SCOTT
    (Enters)
What have you two been doing?

LIZ
Just talking.

JACK
    (Enters with grilling spatula)
Liz, do you like chicken or beef?

LIZ
Beef.

DINA
Beefy.
    (DINA and LIZ laugh)

JACK
That's funny?

SCOTT
    (Lifting empty bottle of wine)
Lizzy thinks everything's funny after a few drinks. Even me. Right, Liz?

LIZ
That's not true.

SCOTT
Liz, did you try this guac?
(SCOTT takes a handful of guacamole)
It's delicious.

LIZ
What did I tell you?

SCOTT
Liz been telling you about her new job?

JACK
Liz, you got a new job?

DINA
No!

SCOTT
She didn't tell you about her new job? Lizzy tells everybody about her new job!

LIZ
No talking shop! Not tonight! I just want to, uh, eat this delicious guacamole. With chips.
(LIZ deliberately takes a large scoop of guacamole)

DINA
Oh, shoot, Jack, can you take the cheesecake out of the freezer? I want to serve it for dessert. Oh!
(DINA convulses with laughter)

                    JACK
Deen, you okay?

                    DINA
Frozen. Cheesecake.

                    LIZ
Frozen cheesecake!
        (LIZ is convulsed)

SCOTT and JACK stare helplessly as LIGHTS FADE.

Scene 2

It is the next morning. DINA and JACK are in the living room. JACK is bent over the crossword puzzle, tapping his pencil on the table.

>DINA

Can you stop that?

>JACK

Stop what?

>DINA

That tapping.

>JACK

What tapping?

>DINA

>(Groans)

>JACK

Just kidding. Did you have fun last night?

>DINA

I have a headache.

>JACK

I'm surprised Liz was able to eat anything, after the way she attacked the guacamole.
>(JACK gets up and goes to the kitchen. He returns with a cloth to wipe down the table)

What's this?
>(JACK holds up the picture of Mr. X.)

                         DINA
            (Snatches it away from him)
Nothing. Jesus.

                         JACK
Seriously, who is this?

                         DINA
It's one of Liz's clients. I'll mail it back to her.

                         JACK
What kind of client? International supermodel?
            (JACK sucks in his cheekbones and strikes a pretentious
            pose)

                         DINA
Stop it.

                         JACK
What?
            (JACK strikes the pose again)
Come on, Dina, where's your sense of humor? You think this guy is good-looking?

                         DINA
He happens to be very smart. Well educated.

                         JACK
Whatever.

                         DINA
Where's the aspirin?

JACK

Top shelf above the dishwasher.

(DINA exits. The doorbell rings)

JACK

I'll get it.

(DINA enters. Sits back on couch)

JACK

Dina, did you order something from — what? The Cerebral Sperm Bank?

DINA

What?

(DINA snatches the box out of JACK'S hand)

JACK

What the hell is that?

DINA

Nothing.

JACK

Really? The Cerebral Sperm Bank sent you nothing?

DINA

It — it must be a wrong address.

JACK

It's addressed to you! Dina Sanborn! What the hell, Dina?

DINA
I don't know.

JACK
You don't know? The Cerebral Sperm Bank sent you a package and you don't know what it is?

DINA
It might be sperm.

JACK
You think?

DINA
Probably.

JACK
And why would the Cerebral Sperm Bank be sending you sperm, Dina?

DINA
(Silent)

JACK
Why would they be sending you sperm? Answer me?

DINA
I want a baby.

JACK
You want a baby.

DINA
(Nods)

JACK
I thought that's what we were doing.

DINA
I was doing.

JACK
Oh, I'm sorry, were you having sex alone?

DINA
No.

JACK
What is this? What's going on?

DINA
I want — to get pregnant.

JACK
(Waits expectantly)

DINA
It's been a year and a half, Jack.

JACK
I'm sorry. I didn't realize there was a timeline on this.

DINA
Jack, I'm 41! Almost 42! How much time do you think I have?

JACK
So you order sperm through the mail?

DINA
I didn't order it.

JACK
THEN WHY IS IT ADDRESSED TO YOU?

DINA
Stop yelling at me!

JACK
I'm sorry, Dina. This is upsetting. What's wrong with my sperm?

DINA
Nothing!

JACK
Then why did you order sperm through the mail?

DINA
I told you, I didn't order it.

JACK
What, they just —

DINA
It was free.

JACK
Free.

DINA
Yeah.

JACK

You mean to tell me they give free sperm samples through the mail? Like with the Sunday paper, only instead of shampoo, you get SPERM?

DINA

Well — that's not quite it.

JACK
(Sarcastically)
Really?

DINA

Look, I did it as a favor.

JACK

As a favor? You ordered sperm as a favor?

DINA

I didn't order —

JACK

Oh, that's right. You didn't order it. It came as a sample, through the mail.

DINA

Sort of.

JACK

So if I go next door, the neighbors would also have received a sperm sample through the mail, right?

DINA

I don't think so.

JACK

What did you say?

DINA

I don't think so.

JACK

No shit.

DINA

I did it as a favor to Liz.

JACK

Oh. Is Liz trying to have a baby? Scott didn't say anything — oh. Oh, I get it. That's not right, Dina.

DINA

What's not —

JACK

You can't keep this from Scott. If Liz is trying to have a baby that's not his, he needs to know about it.
    (JACK reaches for the telephone)

DINA

No!

JACK

Seriously? You want me not to tell him? If it were my wife trying to have a baby with some other guy's sperm, I'd want to know.

DINA

It's not for Liz.

JACK

Dina, what the hell? Why am I holding a sperm sample that's addressed to you that's supposed to help Liz? You're not making much sense here.

DINA

I know.
    (DINA sits)

JACK

So what's going on?

DINA

The sperm was for me. Sort of. It's from Liz's company.

JACK

The Cerebral Sperm Bank?

DINA

No. The Unborn Children of America.

JACK

    (Waits expectantly)

DINA

There's this guy — well, him.
    (DINA gestures towards the picture)

JACK

Wait a minute — you know this guy?

DINA

No. But that's his sperm.

JACK
Why is this guy sending you his sperm?

DINA
Liz set it up.

JACK
Liz is a sperm broker?

DINA
No. She — she helps people conceive.

JACK
But you don't need help.

DINA
How do you know?

JACK
Dina, you have me! Right?

DINA
How badly do you really want a baby? It's not as if you're all that invested!

JACK
That's not true! When have I ever refused you, Dina?

DINA
That's just sex, Jack! You're always up for sex. You're just not up for a baby.

JACK
We're not using anything, Dina! What more do you want me to do?

DINA

I want you to give a shit, that's all! I get the feeling that you don't really care one way or another!

JACK

What, and your little mail order baby daddy here does?

DINA

Yes! Yes, he does! He desperately wants a baby, Jack. This man is educated, attractive. He comes from a good family. He desperately wants to have a baby, and is afraid he won't find the right woman.

JACK

How do you know?

DINA

Why else would he donate his sperm to Liz's company? The man wants progeny and is terrified that it isn't going to happen! Just like me!
    (DINA starts to cry)

JACK

So you thought that maybe the two of you would have a kid?

DINA

At least he wants a kid!

JACK

    (Silence)

DINA

Well?

JACK

(Fuming)

DINA

Aren't you going to say anything?

JACK

I don't know, Dina. I thought you loved me.

DINA

I do.

JACK

Really?

DINA

I just want a baby.

JACK

I thought you wanted my baby. Our baby.

DINA

I do. I'm — I'm just afraid it's not going to happen.

JACK

You really want a baby that badly?

DINA

(Nods)

JACK

Even if it's not mine?

DINA
I just — he seemed so sincere.

JACK
Dina, he's a sperm sample.

DINA
I know……

JACK
(Stands up to leave)
So you don't think my sperm is gonna make it, huh?

DINA
Jack.
    (DINA goes to him and tries to hug him)
It'll still be your baby. Our baby. No one will have to know.

JACK
Okay, Dina.
    (JACK walks to door)

DINA
Where are you going?

JACK
I love you, Dina, but I need to clear my head.
    (JACK leaves)

DINA
(Picks up the package of sperm and hugs it, tearfully.

LIGHTS OUT)

Scene 3

It is later in the morning. DINA is lying on the living room couch, sleeping with the sperm container. JACK is offstage, making breakfast.

JACK

Eggs?

DINA

Really?

JACK

Yup.

DINA

Sure. Thanks.
    (DINA goes to sit. At the table, she notices a photo of a woman)
Who's this?

JACK

Ta-da!
    (JACK takes a package out of the cupboard and places it in front of DINA)
Eggs!

LIZ

The Poached Egg Bank? What's this?

JACK

My contribution to the solution.

DINA
Really?

JACK
Yup. She's pretty, isn't she?

DINA
Yeah, if you like kids. How old is she?

JACK
22. She speaks six languages and is a PhD candidate in world literature.

DINA
Oh, please. And she's 22?

JACK
She was double promoted twice. Very brainy girl. Brazilian.

DINA
That's disgusting.

JACK
Why is it disgusting? She's beautiful. If you get to have his baby, then it's only fair that I get to have hers.

DINA
WHAT?

JACK
What's the big deal?

DINA
I didn't say I was going to have sex with Mr. X!

JACK

Who?

DINA

You know — the sperm donor.

JACK

Mr. X?

DINA

I don't know his name!

JACK

Whose idea was it to call him Mr. X? Liz's?

DINA

What difference does it make? The point is, I'm not sleeping with him.

JACK

Oh — wait a minute. Is that what you think? That I'm going to *sleep* with this woman?

DINA

Isn't that what you meant?

JACK

You think — no!
    (JACK laughs)
That's funny!

DINA

You're not gonna sleep with her?

JACK
Of course not!

DINA
Oh. That's good.
    (Pause)
So it was just a joke?

JACK
No! I'm totally serious about this!
    (JACK puts the Poached Egg box on Dina's plate)

DINA
I don't get it. The Poached Egg Bank. Is breakfast in here?

JACK
Her eggs are in here, Dina.

DINA
You want me to put her eggs —

JACK
Exactly.

DINA
How dare you. There's nothing wrong with my eggs!

JACK
How do you know?

DINA
You know why!

JACK

That was a long time ago, Dina. That was before we met, for chrissakes.

DINA

Not that long —

JACK

You were — 22, right? Same age as this girl!

DINA

This is low!

JACK

You're 41. What makes you think this infertility thing is my fault?

DINA

Who said anything about infertility?

JACK

That's what it is, isn't it?

DINA

That's a pretty strong word —

JACK

Mr. X doesn't think so.

DINA

Don't you tell me what Mr. X thinks!

JACK

I just thought maybe we shouldn't rule out the option of a donor egg, that's all.

DINA

No.

JACK

She's got good genes.

DINA

Absolutely not.

JACK

Why not? It's only fair. You have one with him, then we'll have one with her.

DINA

But —

JACK

Or we could do a little mix — her egg with his sperm. Get it over with in one shot.

DINA

Oh my God, you are sick.

JACK

Why? I thought you wanted this.

DINA

This is about a baby, Jack. Our baby.

JACK

I thought it was about his baby
    (Points to Mr. X)

DINA

He was about our baby.

JACK

Your mean your baby.

DINA

Well if you think you're gonna shoot me up with Miss Brazil, you're wrong.

JACK

She's not gonna hurt you, Dina. It's a very gentle process.

DINA

Fuck you.
  (She goes to the counter and mixes herself a Bloody Mary)

JACK

It's ten in the morning!

DINA

See what you make me do?

JACK

Don't blame me!

DINA

You bring this — this slut into our home and you expect me to take it lying down?

JACK

Oh, I'm sorry. Mr. X — or is that Mr. X-rated — doesn't count?

                    DINA
Jack, I brought him in for *us*.

                    JACK
I don't want a threesome, Dina!
          (JACK broods. DINA drinks)

                    JACK
This is about *him*, isn't it?

                    DINA
Who?

                    JACK
You know who.

                    DINA
Mr. X?

                    JACK
No. Mr. Y. As in why, Dina?

                    DINA
Who are you talking about?

                    JACK
The jerk.

                    DINA
What jerk?

                    JACK
The jerk who knocked you up.

DINA
This has no relation to him. Why would you even think —

JACK
I don't know. He was smart, right?

DINA
Shut up.

JACK
Well, wasn't he?

DINA
I don't want to talk about it.

JACK
Why else would you bring this guy into our marriage?

DINA
It has nothing to do with —

JACK
Was he good looking like him?

DINA
I haven't thought about it.

JACK
Did his face remind you of his or something?

DINA
Please stop.

JACK
Did it?

DINA
I don't know.

JACK
You don't know?

DINA
Maybe. Maybe a little. I didn't think about it. No. Mr. X has a nicer face.

JACK
Do you regret it, Dina?

DINA
What?

JACK
Not marrying him? Having the kid?

DINA
It wasn't an option.

JACK
You could have —

DINA
No.

JACK
But maybe you could have —

                              DINA
Uh uh.

                              JACK
Oh. Sorry.

                              DINA
That's okay.
         (Takes sip of Bloody Mary)
What about her?

                              JACK
Who?

                              DINA
Her? Miss — Egg.

                              JACK
What about her?

                              DINA
Who does she remind you of?

                              JACK
         (Studies picture)
I dunno.

                              DINA
She's got to remind you of someone.

                              JACK
Mmmm. Now that you mention it, she kind of does remind me a little of the exchange student we had senior year.

DINA

Really?

JACK

Yeah. A little around the nose and mouth. I can see it. Yeah. Bianca. Bianca Minaguez.

DINA

Bianca Minaguez. You never told me about her.

JACK

(Shrugs)

DINA

What was she like?

JACK

I don't know. Friendly. Nice. Very pretty. Very very pretty.

DINA

Did you ask her out?

JACK

(Laughs)

DINA

Well? Did you?

JACK

Nope.

DINA

Why not?

JACK

I already had a girlfriend.

DINA

Oh, that's right — Belle, right? Belle what's-her-name.

JACK

Belle what's-her-name.

DINA

What was her name?

JACK

Belle Pattison.

DINA

Belle Pattison.

JACK

(Nods)

DINA

Belle Pattison wanted to marry you.

JACK

She did.

DINA

But you were in love with — Bianca?

JACK

(Shakes head)

                    DINA
You were waiting to graduate college?

                    JACK
I was waiting to meet you.

                    DINA
You didn't even know me.

                    JACK
But I wanted to.

                    DINA
You did not —

                    JACK
I wish I had known you. I would have married you, Dina.

                    DINA
You did marry me, Jack.

                    JACK
I would have married you anyway. When you needed me to.

                    DINA
But then it wouldn't have been *your* baby.

                    JACK
I guess I must have really loved you, then. Before I met you.

                    DINA
    (Smiles)

JACK

You really want Mr. X's baby?

DINA

I want a baby, Jack. I just wish it could be yours.

JACK

What if it's not me?

DINA

I don't know.

JACK

We have her, right?

DINA

I guess…

JACK

Or do we just wing it?

DINA

I guess…

(as LIGHTS FADE)

END OF PLAY

Parents of Typical Children

Parents of Typical Children
Cast of Characters

MRS. DOWNER: A middle-class, well-educated pregnant woman in her early forties.

MR. DOWNER: A middle-class, well-educated man in his early forties.

DR. LAUREL: A middle-class, attractive woman, 30-45.

Scene

A doctor's office in an ultrasound laboratory.

Time

The present.

Setting: A doctor's office in an ultrasound laboratory.

At Rise: It is 11:00 in the morning. MR. and MRS. DOWNER are awaiting the results of MRS. DOWNER'S ultrasound. MRS. DOWNER is seated; MR. DOWNER paces nervously.

MR. DOWNER
What's taking them so long?

MRS. DOWNER
I don't know.
    (Pause)
Could you please try and relax? You're making me tense.

MR. DOWNER
I'm sorry, sweetheart. I, uh — I'm just nervous, that's all. It's normal to be nervous, isn't it?

MRS. DOWNER
Of course it is. It's nerve-wracking, really. All this waiting around.

MR. DOWNER
I mean, really. How long does it take?
    (He looks at watch)
I've got Dawson coming in for a meeting at 1:00.

MRS. DOWNER
Relax. You have plenty of time.

MR. DOWNER

Yeah, yeah. Easy for you to say. Aw, I'm sorry. I just — I just hope everything is okay, that's all.

MRS. DOWNER

It will be. How could it not be? I mean, look at us! We're smart, we're successful, we earn decent salaries —

(DR. LAUREL enters)

DR. LAUREL

Good morning, Mr. and Mrs.
    (Glances at clipboard)
Downer. I'm Dr. Laurel, Head of Genetics at Mercy Clinic.

MR. DOWNER
(Shakes DR. LAUREL'S hand)
Stan Downer. And this is my wife, Vivian.

MRS. DOWNER

How do you do.
    (Shakes DR. LAUREL'S hand.)

DR. LAUREL

I'm sure you're anxious to hear the results of your ultrasound.

MRS. DOWNER

Very.

MR. DOWNER

Extremely.

DR. LAUREL
Okay. Well, let's start with the obvious. Am I correct in assuming that you wanted to know the sex of the baby?

MRS. DOWNER
Yes.

MR. DOWNER
Absolutely.
    (They hold hands anxiously)

DR. LAUREL
Well, you're having a little boy.

MRS. DOWNER
    (Gasps.)

MR. DOWNER
A boy!

MRS. DOWNER
I can't believe it, honey. A little boy!

MR. DOWNER
    (Takes handkerchief out of pocket and blows nose noisily.)

DR. LAUREL
I'm glad you're pleased.

MRS. DOWNER
A boy! Oh, I hope he looks like his Daddy!

MR. DOWNER
Me too.

MRS. DOWNER
Is he — is he — is everything alright with him?

DR. LAUREL
For the most part.

MR. DOWNER
What do you mean?

MRS. DOWNER
Oh my God! Is my baby okay?
  (She stands up)

DR. LAUREL
Mrs. Downer, please try and relax. Your baby is perfectly healthy.

MRS. DOWNER
  (Sits limply)
Thank God.

MR. DOWNER
He's not — he's not — you know the word I mean — not *special* — is special the PC word for —

DR. LAUREL
Your baby does not have Down's Syndrome, no.

MR. DOWNER
Down's Syndrome! That's the phrase I was looking for.

MRS. DOWNER

So the baby's okay.

DR. LAUREL

Well, we ran the standard genetic projection tests — looks, intelligence, athletic ability — and it looks like your boy is going to be a typical child.

MRS. DOWNER

A *typical* child?

MR. DOWNER

What exactly is a typical child?

DR. LAUREL

Average looks, average intelligence — a typical child.

MRS. DOWNER

Are you telling me that my son is going to be average?

MR. DOWNER

There must be some mistake. Are you sure you checked the right fetus?

DR. LAUREL

Mr. Downer, Mrs. Downer, relax. He's a perfectly normal —

MR. DOWNER

 (Glowering)
Average —

DR. LAUREL

—average boy.

MRS. DOWNER
But what does that mean? Average?

DR. LAUREL
You know — typical.

MRS. DOWNER
I don't know what to say.
    (Covers face with hands)

MR. DOWNER
Vivian —
    (Puts hand on MRS. DOWNER'S shoulder)
Look, Dr. Laurel, we make decent money. We're good people. What if we buy him the right education? Something Ivy track — St. Bernard's to start, then maybe Exeter —

DR. LAUREL
Mr. Downer, to be frank with you, I don't know if your son's IQ would be up to the task.

MRS. DOWNER
    (Gasps)
Doctor, how low is it?

DR. LAUREL
Looking at the tests, I'd say around 105.

MR. DOWNER
105? That's impossible!

MRS. DOWNER
Absurd!

MR. DOWNER
Where does it say that?

DR. LAUREL
(Reading from clipboard)
"According to the results of the Greenlough-Finneran scale, the boy's IQ will be no less than 100 and no greater than 110."

MR. DOWNER
I don't know what to say.

MRS. DOWNER
I'm in a state of shock.

DR. LAUREL
I could set up a session with a social worker on staff.

MR. DOWNER
Social worker! Do we look like the kind of people who could use a social worker?
(Turns to wife)
This is all your fault.

MRS. DOWNER
My fault! How is this my fault?

MR. DOWNER
You had that glass of wine right at the beginning, remember? Before we found out.

MRS. DOWNER
Oh, one glass of wine! That wouldn't —

MR. DOWNER
(To DR. LAUREL)
And throughout this entire first trimester, she's had a cup of coffee every day! How's that for taking care of your unborn child?

MRS. DOWNER
Don't you dare make me feel guilty about the coffee! I researched it online, and —

DR. LAUREL
Please. Mr. Downer, Mrs. Downer. One glass of wine did not cause your child's IQ to be typical. Nor did the daily cup of coffee.

MR. DOWNER
Are you saying it's my fault?

DR. LAUREL
I'm not saying it's anyone's fault. It's genetic. Pure and simple. Genetic.

MRS. DOWNER
Stan, this is all your gene pool.

MR. DOWNER
My gene pool? Why is this *my* gene pool?

MRS. DOWNER
Oh, come on Stan. Your father?

MR. DOWNER
What about my father?

MRS. DOWNER
How many times was he passed over for promotion in that accounting firm?

MR. DOWNER
That had nothing to do with his IQ!

MRS. DOWNER
What was it then, the way he dressed?

MR. DOWNER
You leave my father out of this! Besides, what about your cousin Marv?

MRS. DOWNER
Marv?
    (Addresses DR. LAUREL)
Do you believe him? Marv is my third cousin, for chrissake. His DNA is completely different. Right?

MR. DOWNER
Marv is *special.*

MRS. DOWNER
Oh, come on, Stan. Cousin Janie was 47 when she had him.

MR. DOWNER
You're 43!
    (Addresses DR. LAUREL)
Is this an age thing? Have we waited too long for this?

DR. LAUREL
Mr. Downer, Mrs. Downer, you need to relax. As I've said before, there's nothing you could have done to change the outcome of this baby's genetic makeup.

MRS. DOWNER

How can my baby be a typical child? I don't understand it. I always got good grades.

(Turns to MR. DOWNER)

Right before I met you I'd been thinking of getting a Ph.D. Maybe you should have encouraged me more. Typical sexist male.

MR. DOWNER

Me? Sexist? Oh, that's funny, Vivian. Very funny. If I'm so sexist, then *I'll* quit my job when the baby's born and *you* go out and bring home the bacon.

MRS. DOWNER

I don't think so, Stan. What will the neighbors think? None of the other fathers stay home. You know damn well there's a retroactive trend going on for women who want to stay home, and I need to be on top of it.

DR. LAUREL

What do you do for work, Mrs. Downer?

MRS. DOWNER

I'm a public health advocate for women's rights.

DR. LAUREL

You might feel differently after the baby's born. Maybe you could work part time —

MRS. DOWNER

Dr. Laurel! I can't believe you're saying this, just minutes after telling me that my baby will be born a typical child! This baby is going to need all the help it can get! Oh my God.

(Pause)

Can you recommend any courses I should take for dealing with something like this?

DR. LAUREL

Well, there's —

MR. DOWNER

Vivian, we might have to rethink this.

MRS. DOWNER

Rethink what?

MR. DOWNER

This whole thing.

MRS. DOWNER

What whole thing?

MR. DOWNER

This whole baby thing.

MRS. DOWNER

What are you saying?

MR. DOWNER

We might want to give it up.
 (Addresses DR. LAUREL)
Dr. Laurel, what are our options?

DR. LAUREL

Well, there are several options. This test was done early enough so that if you like, you can terminate the pregnancy. This is not a decision that we encourage you to take without serious reflection.

MR. DOWNER

Will it hurt my wife?

DR. LAUREL
It's day surgery. They use a local anesthesia, so it's not painful. There might be some cramping afterwards, and perhaps some heavy bleeding, but your wife won't be in any danger, if that's what you're thinking.

MR. DOWNER
What's our other option?

DR. LAUREL
Adoption.

MRS. DOWNER
Are there people out there who would actually want a typical child?

DR. LAUREL
There are people out there who would welcome a typical child.

MR. DOWNER
What kind of people?

DR. LAUREL
Typical people.

MRS. DOWNER
I don't want typical people raising my baby.

MR. DOWNER
But honey, maybe he'll feel more comfortable.

MRS. DOWNER
I couldn't leave him with a typical family. I don't care if he's one of them. He's still my son. I mean, Stan, we didn't wait this long to have a child so that he could be sent to public school.

MR. DOWNER
I know. But we didn't know he'd be typical.

MRS. DOWNER
What if they're the type of family who take him to Epcot and tell him that it's Europe?

MR. DOWNER
Honey, don't torture yourself.

MRS. DOWNER
I can't do it. I can't do it, Stan.
    (MR. DOWNER puts his arm around her. They are silent.)

MR. DOWNER
Dr. Laurel, what kind of life will our typical child have? What can we realistically expect from him?

DR. LAUREL
I'm glad you asked. I'd like to say first of all that I know how hard this must be for you. Believe me. I have an eight-year old who's a typical child.

MRS. DOWNER
Really? Why didn't you say so?

DR. LAUREL
This really isn't about me. Besides, I find that most parents upon hearing the news, have a lot of grief and anger to express.

MR. DOWNER
How does your husband feel about it?

DR. LAUREL
Ex-husband. It was a relationship that started when I was a freshman in high school, and well, let's just say my taste was not all that discriminating. I was young.

MRS. DOWNER
Was he abusive?

DR. LAUREL
No. Nothing like that. He was just — well, average. He was a jock. Which, by the way, you might be interested to know that a lot of typical children have a higher than average propensity towards athletics.

MRS. DOWNER
Oh!

MR. DOWNER
I didn't know that.

DR. LAUREL
It's true. My little girl is an incredible gymnast. Anyway, her Dad was just an average guy. Ended up going to a state college, getting a job in an accounting firm. Perfectly nice man. Just not the right image I needed to keep me going.

MR. DOWNER
We understand.

MRS. DOWNER
So is your little girl okay?

DR. LAUREL
She's fine. She's healthy, she loves gym class, she's a solid B student — well, I have to push her. She's not really the studious type. Excuse me.
(Dabs her eyes with a Kleenex)
She'll never go to med school, or even graduate school, but with a little perseverance I might be able to get her in a private university where she can hopefully join a sorority and meet the right man. She's very pretty. She'll make someone a nice little wife someday.

MRS. DOWNER
That doesn't sound so bad.

DR. LAUREL
No.
(Dabs eyes, sits straighter)
Let's get back to your son. So. You'll need to know what to expect if you decide to keep him.

MRS. DOWNER
We're keeping him.

MR. DOWNER
(Starts to speak, the changes his mind. Clears throat.)
That's right. We're, uh, keeping him.

DR. LAUREL
Okay. Well, then. As I've already told you, your child will be a boy, average looks, average intelligence, IQ no less than 100 but no greater than 110. What else would you like to know?

MR. DOWNER
What kind of a professional life do you think he'll have?

89

DR. LAUREL
Let's see.
(Picks up clipboard and reads)
"This typical child will probably fall into one or more categories of employment: Sales, Retail, Hospitality, or Physical Education."

MR. DOWNER
Jesus.
(Puts head in his hands.)

MRS. DOWNER
Who's going to love him?

DR. LAUREL
(reading from clipboard)
"This typical child, like most, will have no problem finding a compatible mate through his workplace, a bar, or high school".

MRS. DOWNER
Wow.

MR. DOWNER
It was never that easy for me.

MRS. DOWNER
Maybe his life won't be so bad, after all. At least he'll have a mate.

MR. DOWNER
God knows he won't have a career.

MRS. DOWNER
Somebody's got to teach phys ed. What about the arts? Will he — appreciate them?

DR. LAUREL
(Shrugs and gestures hopelessly)
I can read you the report. "This typical child may enjoy dinner theater and the Blue Man Group."

MRS. DOWNER
(Sags visibly)
Oh.

DR. LAUREL
Mr. Downer, Mrs. Downer — there is a support group that you might be interested in called Parents of Typical Children. The group meets once a month to discuss common issues and goals, and really, it's an informative and relaxing way to be around people who are going through the same thing. Here's their brochure.

MRS. DOWNER
I don't think I could do that.

MR. DOWNER
What if I know someone in the group and it got back to my office that my child was — typical? I'd never live that down. Never.

DR. LAUREL
The group is very protective of anonymity, believe me. Don't you think that the other Parents of Typical Children feel the same way about it as you do?

MRS. DOWNER
I can't — I can't submit like that. No.
(She stands up)

MR. DOWNER
Where are you going?

MRS. DOWNER

I'm going to go home, put on some classical music with the stereo speaker next to my womb, and read some Shakespeare aloud. Something fun, like "Midsummer's".

MR. DOWNER

Seriously?

DR. LAUREL

Mrs. Downer —

MRS. DOWNER

I've heard about all I can take. First of all, I don't believe you. No child of mine will ever be born typical. That's just not in the cards.

DR. LAUREL

But the report —

MRS. DOWNER

There's margin for error.

MR. DOWNER

That's true. How certain are these reports, anyway?

DR. LAUREL

Well, nothing is 100%, but there's a pretty strong chance —

MR. DOWNER

How strong?

DR. LAUREL

98%.

MRS. DOWNER

98%!

MR. DOWNER

(Overlapping)
So there's a 2% chance he's above average!

MRS. DOWNER

You didn't tell us that!

MR. DOWNER

This test is baloney. We're leaving.

DR. LAUREL

Fine. You don't have to believe the report, or the fact that it's 98% accurate. But in eight years' time, when your son has to be forced to read a book, can't distinguish between a viola and a French horn and would rather play baseball than go to the Met, you may want this.
    (Holds out brochure)
Parents of Typical Children.

MRS. DOWNER

No. Thank you Dr., but no.
    (She takes brochure, rips it in two, throws it on the floor.
    MR. and MRS. DOWNER exit)

DR. LAUREL

(Sighs)

MR. DOWNER

(from offstage)
Vivian, I think I left something in the doctor's office. I'll be right back.
    (He runs into the office)

MR. DOWNER, continued
May I?
(He gestures to the brochure)

DR. LAUREL
(Nods.)

MR. DOWNER
(Picks up brochure halves and puts them in his jacket.
He looks at DR. LAUREL and smiles ruefully.)
I've, uh — I've always wanted to see the Blue Man Group.

(He exits as LIGHTS FADE.)

END OF PLAY

The Octomom Conceives

The Octomom Conceives
Cast of Characters

WOMAN: A mother of six, 30 -40 years of age, attractive, with long hair and make-up. She wears a hospital gown.

DOCTOR: A handsome man, 30-45, wearing a lab coat over chinos and a button-down shirt.

NURSE: A woman, anywhere from 25 — 50, dressed in a nurse's uniform

MOTHER: A woman, attractive but tough, anywhere from 50 — 75. She is the mother of WOMAN, and is often stuck taking care of WOMAN's kids. She is dressed carelessly, in a brightly colored tracksuit.

Scene

A fertility clinic in California.

Time

The present.

Setting: The post-surgery room of a fertility clinic.

At Rise: A gurney is in the middle of the room. WOMAN is lying in the middle, DOCTOR by her side.

                    WOMAN
(Groans)

                    DOCTOR
Good morning.

                    WOMAN
Where am I?

                    DOCTOR
Seriously?

                    WOMAN
(Holds head)
Oh, God.

                    DOCTOR
I think this went very well.

                    WOMAN
What are you talking about?
    (sees syringe next to her)
Oh my God.

DOCTOR
You remember.

WOMAN
Oh God.

DOCTOR
You looked like you were enjoying yourself.

WOMAN
Did I?

DOCTOR
I'd say so.

WOMAN
Was anyone with me?

DOCTOR
Excuse me?

WOMAN
Was anyone — with me?

DOCTOR
Well —

WOMAN
When I came in? Was anyone with me?

DOCTOR
No, you came alone.

WOMAN
Shoot.

DOCTOR
Is something wrong?

WOMAN
(Groans)
I think I need to make a phone call.

DOCTOR
The nurse will bring you your things.

WOMAN
Thank you.
(She sits up, looks around, lies back down. She bolts up again)
Doctor, did I go through with the procedure?

DOCTOR
What kind of question is that?

WOMAN
I just —

DOCTOR
Of course you went through with the procedure. Very nicely, I might add. You were very cooperative. And quite cheerful!

WOMAN
Who did I pick?

DOCTOR
Excuse me?

                    WOMAN
Who did I pick?

                    DOCTOR
You really don't remember?

                    WOMAN
No.

                    DOCTOR
            (Picks up catalog)
This one. Right here.

                    WOMAN
Huh.
            (Reads description as NURSE comes in, carrying a handbag and clothes)
Wait a minute. It says here that he's 5'7".

                    DOCTOR
That's right.

                    NURSE
5'7".
            (NURSE starts to laugh. DOCTOR joins in)

                    WOMAN
What's so funny?

                    DOCTOR
Oh, nothing.

                    NURSE
You were just so practical about it. Remember?

NURSE, continued
(NURSE pokes DOCTOR)
You said that you wanted a little guy so that the baby wouldn't be that heavy, because you were just a little thing yourself.
(NURSE laughs appreciatively)

DOCTOR
We don't always encounter patients who are that practical. Everyone always wants the big ones.

NURSE
Oh, I know. 'Give me someone 6'10"'. And blonde.

DOCTOR
We should really charge more for height.

NURSE
Not you. You picked a small dark one. Cute.

WOMAN
I need to make a phone call.

NURSE
Who are you going to call?

WOMAN
My mother.
(She lies back)
My mother is going to kill me.

NURSE
I spoke to your mom a few minutes ago. She's on her way.

WOMAN
(Sits up)
You called my mother?

DOCTOR
Now just a minute —

NURSE
You told us to! Didn't she, Doctor?

DOCTOR
You certainly did.

WOMAN
When?

NURSE
Last night, when you were filling out the forms. We asked — we always ask —

DOCTOR
Yes we do.

NURSE
"Who would you like us to call?" and you told us your mother!

WOMAN
Oh my God. How drunk was I?

NURSE
You didn't seem too bad.

DOCTOR
I couldn't tell.

WOMAN
I barely remember —

MOTHER
(Offstage)
Where's my daughter?

WOMAN
Oh God, she's gonna kill me.

MOTHER
Where are you?

NURSE
In here, Mum.

MOTHER
(Storms in)

DOCTOR
I think I'll go check on some other patients.

MOTHER
Oh no you don't.

DOCTOR
Is something the matter?

MOTHER
Something the matter? Is he kidding?

WOMAN
Mom……

NURSE

I think you should —

MOTHER

(To WOMAN)
Did you go through with it?

WOMAN

(Hangs her head)

MOTHER

Were you drunk?

WOMAN

(mumbles)

MOTHER

What? I can't hear you.

WOMAN

I said maybe a little.

MOTHER

Maybe a little. That's great. That's just great.
    (To DOCTOR)
So you let her come in here, knowing that she was three sheets to the wind, and you let her make a baby?

DOCTOR

She didn't seem that bad to me…

NURSE

I checked her in. I thought she seemed fine.

MOTHER
(To WOMAN)
Why is it that every time you get drunk you come down here and make a baby?

WOMAN
I don't know.

MOTHER
What do you mean, you don't know? How could you not know?

WOMAN
I don't know. It's like — I just — forget.

MOTHER
Forget what? That you have six other kids at home, all of them born out of a needle?
(MOTHER holds up syringe in disgust)

WOMAN
Don't say that!

MOTHER
Well, it's true!

WOMAN
You make me sound so irresponsible!

DOCTOR
I definitely need to check on my other patients.

MOTHER
Not so fast. Didn't she tell you she has six other kids at home?

DOCTOR
Now that I think of it, she did mention —

MOTHER
And you let her go through with it?

NURSE
Please, Ma'am, if I may, your daughter is a grown woman!

MOTHER
Who has six children by six different little specimens!

WOMAN
Don't call them that!

MOTHER
Speaking of which, who's your latest stud?

NURSE
(points to profile in book. NURSE and DOCTOR start to chuckle)

MOTHER
5'7". Hmm. The baby will be light.

WOMAN
That's what I was thinking.

MOTHER
For once, you used your head. I got six tall, blonde mouths to feed at home. 99th percentile for height, every last one of them.

WOMAN
This one will be small.

MOTHER
That's if it takes. Let's just pray that it doesn't.

DOCTOR
Oh, I think there's a pretty good chance —

MOTHER
Don't you have patients to see?

DOCTOR
Uh, yeah. I do. Pleasure.
    (He holds out is hand for MOTHER to shake. She
    doesn't. To WOMAN)
And you, young lady — next time you get drunk, go home and sleep it off, okay?

WOMAN
I'll try.

DOCTOR
Good girl. Coming, nurse?

NURSE
Yes.
    (To WOMAN)
I'll see you on the way out.
    (They exit)

WOMAN
I'm sorry, Mommy.

MOTHER
You're sorry. What were you thinking?

WOMAN

I like having babies.

MOTHER

Having babies is one thing, but who's going to feed them? My God, girl, you have six at home already!

WOMAN

I was drunk. I'm sorry.

MOTHER

I'm warning you, Missy, this is the last time, if I have to sterilize you myself.

WOMAN

Mom, how can you say that? I'm a wonderful mother. I love my kids.

MOTHER

If you loved them, you would have stopped. A long time ago. What kind of people would let you do this?

WOMAN

I know, I know. This will be the last time. I promise.

MOTHER

You said that the last time.

WOMAN

This time, I really mean it. Really really.

MOTHER

What's so special about this time?

WOMAN
(Averts her head)

MOTHER
What? What are you hiding from me?

WOMAN
Nothing.

MOTHER
Speak up, I can't hear you.

WOMAN
I said, he might have injected more than one.

MOTHER
What did you say?

WOMAN
He might have injected more than one.

MOTHER
How many did he inject? Tell me!

WOMAN
Umm…

MOTHER
Tell me!

WOMAN
Uh…

MOTHER
Doctor! Doctor!

DOCTOR
(Runs in)
Is everything okay?

MOTHER
No, everything is NOT okay! How many eggs did you shoot her up with?

DOCTOR
Now hold on —

WOMAN
Please don't tell her —

MOTHER
How many?

DOCTOR
Madam, you need to change your tone —

MOTHER
(Leans in to DOCTOR menacingly)

DOCTOR
Eight.

MOTHER
EIGHT?

DOCTOR
She was feeling randy.

MOTHER
Eight? Is that even legal? What kind of a doctor are you?

WOMAN
Mummy, please —

MOTHER
Take them out.

WOMAN
NO!

DOCTOR
I can't do that —

MOTHER
Take them out —

WOMAN
Please! Please! Please don't kill my babies!

DOCTOR
Do you have any idea what you're saying?

MOTHER
You bet I do. Take them out.

DOCTOR
That would be completely unethical.

MOTHER
I have six mouths to feed at home. Take them out.

NURSE
(Comes running in)
What's all the fuss?

DOCTOR
I'll handle this. Madam, what you're suggesting is murder, with a capital M. We are in the business here of creating life, not taking it away.

NURSE
You mean she —

DOCTOR
That's right.

NURSE
How could you?

WOMAN
(Sobs quietly. NURSE goes to comfort her while DOCTOR takes MOTHER aside)

DOCTOR
The chances of all eight of these embryos surviving are 1 in 8 million.

MOTHER
Would you bet your medical license on that fact?

DOCTOR
Absolutely.

MOTHER
Fine.
(To WOMAN)
Are you ready to go?

WOMAN
In a minute. I just need a minute.

NURSE
Honey, you take all the time you want.

MOTHER
I have to get home to rest of your kids. Are you okay to drive?

WOMAN
(Nods)

DOCTOR
Stop by the desk to sign your release form before you go.

(DOCTOR and NURSE exit. MOTHER starts to follow, then turns around and kisses WOMAN on the forehead. MOTHER exits)

WOMAN
(Leans back into bed and starts to hum "Lullaby" as LIGHTS FADE)

END OF PLAY

The Dedoption

The Dedoption
Cast of Characters

COCO CHILDS: A famous female movie star. She is beautiful to look at, meticulously dressed, yet there is something cold and slightly detached about her. She is anywhere between 40 to 50 years of age, but should look much younger.

TOM RIDER: A famous male movie star. He is handsome in a boyish, all-American way. Casually, but expensively, dressed, he is warmer than his wife, at least on the surface. He is anywhere between 40 and 50 years of age, but should look much younger.

SYLVIE: The nanny of CoCo and Tom's adopted children. She is a very pretty, fresh-faced nineteen year old girl. She is dressed casually, in jeans, sweater and sneakers, and carries an iPhone.

MRS. BRADY: The founder and president of the agency where CoCo and Tom have come to give back their adopted children. She is expensively and conservatively dressed, attractive in a well-put together way, anywhere between 35 and 60 years of age.

YOUNG WOMAN OR YOUNG MAN: Mrs. Brady's assistant, in his or her early twenties.

<u>Scene</u>

MRS. BRADY's office in Los Angeles, California

<u>Time</u>

The present.

Setting: The large, spacious office of MRS. BRADY, founder and president of the first dedoption agency in Southern California.

At Rise: It is early afternoon. COCO CHILDS, TOM RIDER and their children's nanny, SYLVIE, have just arrived for their appointment with MRS. BRADY.

YOUNG WO/MAN
Please take a seat. Mrs. Brady will be right with you.

COCO
Thank you.

TOM
Thanks very much.
    (To SYLVIE)
Sit.
    (SYLVIE sits, taking a phone out of her pocket. She texts, looking sulky and tearful)
    (To COCO)
Are you sure you want to do this?

COCO
Are you kidding me? What choice do we have?

TOM
I don't know.
    (He runs his fingers through his hair)
There are other options.

COCO
Like what? And don't tell me your sister —

TOM
Hey, my sister came through for us during a very bad time —

COCO
I don't care. She's still your sister.

TOM
What's that supposed to mean?

COCO
It means she's still your sister!

TOM
So what?

COCO
She can be hurtful, that's all.

TOM
My sister has always been a big fan of yours. A big fan.

COCO
She's an even bigger fan of yours.

TOM
We're family!

COCO
Exactly.

TOM
And what does this have to do with the kids?

COCO
It has *everything* to do with the kids, Tom. Everything.

TOM
Do you have to start? Can't you just stop sniping for once?

COCO
I am *not* sniping.

TOM
Listen to yourself! 'I am *not* sniping'. You *are* sniping.

COCO
How is that sniping?

TOM
I don't like your tone.

(Door opens. MRS. BRADY walks in.)

MRS. BRADY
Hello. Deborah Brady. Please to meet you.
(She extends her hand)

TOM
Tom. Tom Rider. And this is my wife —

COCO
Ex-wife.

TOM
Ex-wife —

                    COCO
Actually, not until I sign the papers, darling.
          (COCO, TOM and MRS. BRADY laugh, nervously)

                     TOM
CoCo Childs.

                  MRS. BRADY
Tom. CoCo. A pleasure. And — I just want to say to both of you, that I am a huge fan. Huge.

                     TOM
Thank you.

                    COCO
          (Smiles and nods coldly)

                  MRS. BRADY
And —
          (points to SYLVIE)
- is this one of the children?

                    COCO
No! Are you kidding me?

                  MRS. BRADY
I'm sorry. I didn't —

                     TOM
This is — uh, the nanny. Daisy. Daisy, this is —

                    COCO
Daisy was two nannys ago.

TOM
What? Nobody told me -

COCO
Sylvie.

MRS. BRADY
Nice to meet you, Sylvie.

SYLVIE
(Nods. COCO gestures at her)
Nice to meet you.
(SYLVIE begins texting on the iPhone, after casting a wary eye on the adults)

MRS. BRADY
Is she —

TOM
We thought that Daisy —

COCO
Sylvie.

TOM
(Laughs)
Sylvie might be able to share what she knows about the children. After all, she's been the children's primary caregiver for about -
(To COCO)
When did Daisy leave?

COCO
Daisy left March of last year, followed by Fatima, who left in September, followed by Sylvie.

TOM
Okay. September, October, November, December —
    (TOM counts quietly on his fingers)
Wow, has it already been nine months? Time flies.

MRS. BRADY
Who's with the children now?

TOM
The secondary nanny — uh, what's her —
    (To COCO)
You tell Mrs. Brady, darling. I can't do all of the talking.

COCO
    (Glaring at TOM)
Honor. Honor is with the children.

MRS. BRADY
That's nice. Will she be bringing the children in later?

COCO
Yes.

TOM
That's right.

MRS. BRADY
Okay. Let's start by talking a little bit about the children, okay? There are —
    (MRS. BRADY glances at her file)
—two of them, correct?

COCO
Yes.

                    TOM
Walter and Clover.

                    COCO
Chloe.

                    TOM
Chloe?

                    COCO
She wants to be called Chloe now.

                    TOM
Since when, CoCo?

                    COCO
Since —
         (COCO looks in appeal at MRS. BRADY)

               MRS. BRADY
Let's see what we have on file.
         (MRS. BRADY peers into their folder.)
               MRS. BRADY, continued
Ah. It says here the girl is called Clover.

                    TOM
Clover. I told you.

                    COCO
I thought Chloe would be more — I don't know — appealing, you know?

                    TOM
It's not her name.

SYLVIE
She hates it.

COCO
Sylvie, dear, when we need you to comment, we'll ask you, okay?

(SYLVIE glowers and reluctantly goes back to texting)

COCO
Why can't we call her Chloe?
    (To MRS. BRADY)
Don't you think that Chloe sounds more marketable, more — mainstream?

MRS. BRADY
Oh, I don't know, CoCo. Clover has a nice, old-fashioned ring to it. A little Noel Coward-ish, don't you think?

COCO
I don't know him.

TOM
No. Film or tv?

MRS. BRADY
A little before your time, maybe.
    (Clears throat)
So tell me about the children. Walter and Clover.

COCO
They're nice kids.

TOM
Real nice kids.

MRS. BRADY

Walter is — twelve?

(TOM and COCO look at each other)

TOM

That's right — twelve.

COCO

He's part Eskimo.

MRS. BRADY

How unusual!

TOM

But you wouldn't know it. I mean, he's a sharp dresser. He looks — he looks — well, like us.

COCO

Tom!

MRS. BRADY

Do you mean he resembles you?

TOM

Not really.

COCO

He means he looks white. Walter looks white.

TOM

That's not — yeah, he looks white.

                             COCO
What's that got to do with anything?

                             TOM
Well, Miss Marketability, I think it has a lot to do with everything!

                             COCO
You didn't think so when we got him.

                             TOM
Oh, yes I did. We deliberately picked him for that reason. Our manager at the time —

                             COCO
I don't remember this.

                             TOM
     (Glares at her)
Our manager at the time said it would be good PR.

                             COCO
I don't remember.

                             TOM
Of course not.

                          MRS. BRADY
Okay. So Walter is a nice boy, part Eskimo, a sharp dresser…what else?

                             COCO
He, um — he shares well.

                          MRS. BRADY
He shares well?

                            TOM
What's that supposed to mean? CoCo?

                            COCO
He shares well. He's a *sharer*. He — he brings things home from school. Pictures. Books. And he shares them. He likes to talk about them.

                            TOM
That's not really a quality.

                            MRS. BRADY
I think we can work with that.
         (Writes on notepad)
Shares well. I like that. That's good.

                            COCO
Thank you.

                            MRS. BRADY
Sylvie? Do you have anything to add?

                            SYLVIE
He's really interested in astronomy.
         (TOM and COCO stare at her)

                            COCO
We knew that.

                            TOM
I think it's because of that movie I made in '92 — "Intergalactic Armageddon." That may have had something to do —

SYLVIE
No, it's Mr. Weintraub, his science teacher. He took the class on this really cool -

COCO
Sylvie, you're interrupting.

SYLVIE
Sorry.

MRS. BRADY
So Walter is a boy with hobbies! This is all very good, very good indeed.
    (She writes something on a pad)
Now tell me about the other one. Clover.

COCO
Are you sure you don't want to call her Chloe?

TOM
You heard Mrs. Brady, darling. Clover is very Noel Cowers.

MRS. BRADY
Coward.

TOM
Are you calling me a coward?

MRS. BRADY
Oh no, no. It's Coward. Noel Coward.

TOM
Oh. Coward.
    (Pause)
Did you say he was in film, or television?

SYLVIE
He's a playwright.
    (TOM, COCO and MRS. BRADY stare at her)
My high-school drama club did one of his plays.

MRS. BRADY
Well. Let's get back to Clover, shall we? How old is she?

COCO
Sixteen.

TOM
Fifteen.

COCO
Sixteen.

TOM
Fifteen.

COCO
I thought she was —

TOM
Fifteen.

COCO
How do you know?

TOM
    (To MRS. BRADY)
She's very pretty.

MRS. BRADY

Uh-huh.

COCO

I thought she was sixteen.

TOM

Fifteen. Don't you think you should know how old your daughter is?

COCO

May I remind you that the girl is not my real daughter? I am far too young to have a fifteen year old, never mind sixteen!

TOM

If she were sixteen, I'd know it.
    (To MRS. BRADY)
The girl is beautiful.

MRS. BRADY

    (Encouraging)
Tell me more.

TOM

She's a beauty. A stunner.

COCO

She's okay.

TOM

Seriously? Can you look me in the eye and tell me that that girl is just 'okay'?

COCO

She's okay! I mean, she's sixteen. She's awkward.

TOM
Fifteen.

MRS. BRADY
Sylvie, do you want to weigh in on this?

SYLVIE
(Tears herself away from phone)
What?

MRS. BRADY
How old would you say Clover is?

SYLVIE
I thought she was like, older than me. I mean, hasn't she had surgery?

(TOM and COCO stare at her)

TOM
Who hired this girl?

COCO
Relax, Tom, we won't be needing her after today.

MRS. BRADY
Let's stay on track. I know you're anxious to get this done. Anything else you want to tell me about Clover?

TOM
She loves film premieres of any kind. I think she's much better with the press than Walter is.

COCO
She's like her father.

TOM
We don't know her father, CoCo.

COCO
Oh, very funny. You know who I mean.

MRS. BRADY
How old were the children when you adopted them?

TOM
Ooh, that's a toughie.

COCO
Tom.
  (Pause)
Clover was three months, and Walter was two.

MRS. BRADY
Months?

COCO
No. Two years. Two years. He was very cute.
  (She looks as if she's going to cry. She composes herself)

MRS. BRADY
I'm sure he was. Did you bring your family photo history with you?

TOM
Yup. All of our albums, just like you said.
  (TOM pulls forward a large cardboard box and slides it toward MRS. BRADY, who lifts four photo albums out of the box)

MRS. BRADY

My, this is a lot! Let's see -
    (MRS. BRADY starts to leaf through album, frowning)
There aren't too many of the children alone, are there?

    (SYLVIE leans in, her phone in her hands.)

COCO

No. We're two of the most photographed people in the world! Why would we want pictures of just babies? I mean — who really cares?

MRS. BRADY

Well, in terms of each child's personal physical development, they'll want to have a few photos of themselves as babies. Ah, here's one of — is it Clover? It says 'C, six months'.

TOM

Yup. That's Clover all right.

MRS. BRADY

Wonderful.
    (She pulls photo out of the book.)
Oh, and this must be Walter? 'Boy, around two and a half, on swing' —

COCO

That's him. That's my — that's Walter.

MRS. BRADY

These will do fine.
    (MRS. BRADY flips through the rest of the album and throws it in the wastebasket without closing it)

TOM

Whoa!

COCO

What are you doing?

SYLVIE

(Looks up)

MRS. BRADY

We can't possibly use these.

COCO

Can't we take them home?

MRS. BRADY

I think that's a bad idea, dear.

TOM

But why?

COCO

They're our children —

MRS. BRADY

No, dear. No. I'm sorry, but it has to be this way.

TOM

(Slumping back in seat)
I see your point.

COCO

I don't understand.

MRS. BRADY

You'll have your memories.

COCO

But I want the photos.

MRS. BRADY

I'm afraid it's not possible. It won't be good for you, or for the children.

COCO

They won't even know!

MRS. BRADY

You and Tom live in the public eye. If these photos were ever to come under scrutiny, it would ruin everything we're attempting to do today. For you and for the children.

TOM

She's right, CoCo.

COCO

Fine. Dammit.

TOM

It's not a big —

COCO

It is a big. Very big. I'll never have any shots of me as a young mother again.

>(There is a small thump. Everyone turns to look at SYLVIE, who has dropped her phone into the wastebasket)

SYLVIE

Sorry.

(She takes a minute to retrieve it)

TOM

Who knows, CoCo? Maybe your next husband will *want* kids. And as far as young goes, there's always surgery.

SYLVIE

Me-ow.

COCO

That's very amusing, Tom. Very amusing. I'm surprised you're letting the photos go so easily.

TOM

Why is that, dear?

COCO

I believe you still had all of your original hair when this one was taken.
(COCO grabs album from wastebasket and snatches a photo)

SYLVIE

No way!
(SYLVIE leans forward to see)

MRS. BRADY
(Tugs photo from COCO's hand)
CoCo, dear — may I call you CoCo?

COCO
(Coldly)
Of course.

MRS. BRADY
I know this is hard. If this were easy, more people would be doing it. But believe me, when I tell you that in a year from now, maybe even a few months from now, when you see photos of the children at premieres, or shopping with their parents, or attending sporting events, you won't even recognize them.

TOM
Does your fee include surgery?

MRS. BRADY
Well, no, that's not what I —

TOM
Because if it does, well, we might want to rethink this. I mean, for 15, the girl is really beautiful. And Walter, well, maybe a little around the nose, but —

COCO
Walter is adorable. You leave him alone.

MRS. BRADY
Tom, CoCo, I assure you, the children won't be getting surgery. There's no need to alter their faces.

COCO
Then why won't we be able to recognize them?

MRS. BRADY
Well, the fact that you're here today means that you've already taken the first step towards distancing yourselves from the situation. As I've said before, this is not something that every parent can afford to do. In a few moments I'm going to ask you a series of questions that are actually cognitive exercises designed to help ease the transition. By the end of today's session, you will regain a much

MRS. BRADY, continued
stronger, more independent sense of direction which will set you both firmly on your individual paths.

TOM
(Nods enthusiastically)

COCO
What if my individual path involves someone else?

MRS. BRADY
Um….well, that's fine, as long as that someone else isn't Tom or one of the children.

COCO
No. I wasn't planning on that.

TOM
Why, baby? Who have you got your eyes on this time?

COCO
I'm not saying I have my eyes on anybody.

SYLVIE
Maybe not your eyes.

COCO
What's that supposed to mean?

SYLVIE
Nothing.
(SYLVIE goes back to texting)

COCO
Is it really necessary that she be here?
(indicates SYLVIE)

TOM
Daisy's perceptions could be useful. Right?

MRS. BRADY
Right. For now, Sylvie
(MRS. BRADY glances at TOM)
stays in the room. Is that okay with you, dear?

SYLVIE
Cool.

MRS. BRADY
Now, I'd like to ask you each a few questions. CoCo, let's start with you. When was the first time you realized that you wanted to be a mother?

COCO
Oh God, I remember it like it was yesterday. I can still see the picture of that bi —
(catches herself)
I'm sorry. I was at the dentist's office, waiting to get my teeth whitened, and I picked up a magazine, one of those fashion mags, you know, that features celebrities — like us — and they had this huge photo spread of Maisie Lucas. She had just won the Oscar for that insipid piece of —

SYLVIE
"The Dream is Alive"?

COCO
Ugh. Please.

SYLVIE
That film rocked.

COCO
Spare me your mindless commentary.

TOM
We've had this discussion before, CoCo. I think you're being too harsh on Steve. He directed a really good, really tight —

MRS. BRADY
Back to what you saw in the fashion magazine, CoCo. Something about the fashion magazine made you want to become a mother.

COCO
Yes.......yes. As I said, it was a photo spread of Maisie Lucas, at home with her Oscar. And she was seven months' pregnant, and she looked gorgeous.

TOM
Well, she's a beautiful woman. Beautiful.

COCO
Really. I didn't know you felt that strongly about her.

TOM
No, it's just —

MRS. BRADY
She looked gorgeous. Gorgeous how?

COCO
I don't know. She looked big, and ripe, and her skin was glowing, her hair was perfect —

TOM
CoCo, maybe she just had a really good stylist that day.

COCO
No, it was her. She looked great. And in a little box, you know, one of those little insets, they had a recipe for Maisie's favorite pregnancy dish — some kind of pasta with cheese sauce. Pasta! I can't even remember the last time I had pasta. And there she was, looking gorgeous and eating — pasta.

MRS. BRADY
So you decided to have a baby?

TOM
Uh, not exactly —

MRS. BRADY
Tom, you'll have your turn, I promise.

COCO
Thank you. He always hogs my interviews.

MRS. BRADY
Okay. Back to the baby, and wanting to be a mom.

COCO
Right. Well, I knew I wouldn't actually have a baby. I mean, Maisie looked great, but I'm not stupid — somebody has to take all that weight off after the baby comes. And my options for birth just weren't that great - you know a C-section is fine, you can schedule it, but I read somewhere that your uterus never really shrinks back to where it should be. And the other way — you know, a baby coming through your — you know — no.
(COCO shudders)

COCO, continued
No. I — no.

SYLVIE
She's pretty tight —

COCO
Excuse me?

SYLVIE
—ly wrapped.,

COCO
Thank you for that observation, Sylvie, but why don't you save your comments for the children?

MRS. BRADY
So you decided to adopt.

COCO
Well, yes. Sort of.

TOM
Sort of.

MRS. BRADY
What does 'sort of' mean?

COCO
You've heard of the Carion Group?

MRS. BRADY
Sure. Oh, okay.

                    COCO
The one where they —

                  MRS. BRADY
That's right. The one where they send you a list of all the unwed mothers in the area —

                    TOM
Photos.

                    COCO
Exactly.

                  MRS. BRADY
And you get to pick based on —

                    COCO
Photos, interviews —

                    TOM
Photos. We looked at a lot of photos.

                    COCO
We wanted our children to be pretty. Like us.

                  MRS. BRADY
Of course.

                    COCO
And it was nice. We got to meet with the mother, saw a picture of the father. Carion did an excellent job of handling everything.

MRS. BRADY
I'm sure. They usually do.

TOM
It was first class all the way.

MRS. BRADY
So, after the mother delivered Clover, did you take her home? No, wait, you already told me it was three months before she came home with you.

COCO
That's right. We wanted to make sure she was sleeping through the night before we brought her home.

MRS. BRADY
So she stayed with…the mother?

(TOM and COCO look at each other. TOM shrugs.)

COCO
I gues…I don't know. I mean, that's the kind of thing you pay an agency for.

MRS. BRADY
So true.

COCO
That's the kind of detail I wouldn't want to be bothered with.

MRS. BRADY
Of course not. So tell me, CoCo, what was the hardest part about bringing Clover home?

                    COCO
Well…she was a baby.

                 MRS. BRADY
Yes.

                    COCO
Babies don't do much, and yet they're very demanding. I would never have known this, had I not become a mother.

                 MRS. BRADY
They can be very demanding, yes.

                    COCO
Completely. And so helpless! I just wanted to scream, "Get your own bottle" but of course, she couldn't even walk at the time, never mind heat milk.

                 MRS. BRADY
Not very helpful, are they?

                    COCO
And yet, being a mother changed my life completely.

                 MRS. BRADY
Go on, dear.

                    COCO
Tom and I have always been photographed — right, Tom?

                    TOM
It's true. We're big.

SYLVIE
(looks up, rolls eyes)

COCO
But once we brought home Clover, it was different. The photographers were different. They were careful. Almost kind. And the photos themselves were different. More loving, somehow. Tender.

MRS. BRADY
A far cry from the siren that we know you to be.

COCO
(Confused)
Siren?

MRS. BRADY
Well, you know. Temptress. Every man's fantasy woman.

TOM
(Snorts)

COCO
I guess…but I liked it. I've never been a Method actor — Tom and I don't believe in the Method.

TOM
It's crap. Self-indulgent crap. I'm an actor. I act.

COCO
I'm an actor, too. But for the first time, I kind of knew what it was like to "act" like a mother. I was a mother. I didn't have to imagine it. I could really use what I had with Clover in my work.

MRS. BRADY
That's nice —

COCO
And I think that before I had Clover, a lot of producers just didn't see me as the mother type. I was too, how did you put it, too much of a temptress. After Clover came, and a few of the photographs with her were given widespread release, producers started to see me differently. I started to get calls for roles that previously, I hadn't even been considered for.

MRS. BRADY
The young mother roles?

COCO
(Nods)
It was nice.

MRS. BRADY
How hard that must have been, to go from being a seductress, the personal fantasy of every male between the ages of 13 and 85, to becoming a mere mother.

COCO
Oh, I looked good —

MRS. BRADY
But let's be realistic, CoCo. Motherhood isn't sexy.

TOM
She had some really nice outfits made, believe me.

COCO

Thank you.
      (COCO reaches her hand out to TOM, thinks better of it, and pulls it back)

MRS. BRADY

Well, that's all very well and fine when the baby is three months old, but now that Clover is sixteen —

TOM

Fifteen.

MRS. BRADY

Fifteen, she is...
      (looks at photos)
a *stunner*, no? A real beauty.

COCO

      (Dismissively)
She's fine.

MRS. BRADY

She could be a model.

SYLVIE

She wants to model, but she
      (jerks her head towards COCO)
won't let her.

MRS. BRADY

Really? Why not?

COCO

I don't think it would be good for her.

MRS. BRADY
Oh. That's very maternal of you, dear. So it isn't because she's competition.

TOM
There's no competition, believe me.

MRS. BRADY
Good.

COCO
I just don't think models are very healthy, that's all. It's not a healthy environment for a young girl like Chloe — Clover. The whole body-image thing.

(MRS. BRADY, TOM and SYLVIE stare at COCO.)

MRS. BRADY
(Clears throat)
Right.

COCO
But I have to admit, having children did get me over that hurdle between ingénue and young mother.

MRS. BRADY
Has Clover started dating?

TOM
(laughs nervously)
What?

MRS. BRADY
Boys. Has Clover shown an interest in boys yet?

TOM

She's a kid. She's fifteen.

COCO

No. She's much too sheltered. Tom and I are very overprotective. Of both our kids.

SYLVIE

(Snorts)

COCO

It's true.

MRS. BRADY

Sylvie, you've supervised the children on occasion, yes?

SYLVIE

On occasion? Yes.

MRS. BRADY

So would you say that Clover is interested in boys?

COCO

How would Sylvie know?

TOM

Out of the question.

MRS. BRADY

Sylvie?

SYLVIE

She has a boyfriend.

TOM
(Stands)
What?

COCO
You're making this up.

SYLVIE
She has a boyfriend.

TOM
Why would you say such a vile thing about my — daughter?

SYLVIE
It's true.

COCO
How would you know?

SYLVIE
CoCo, when was the last time you spent more than two consecutive hours with your kids?

COCO
Quality time, Sylvie.
    (To MRS. BRADY)
It's called quality time for a reason. You don't hear anyone refer to it as quantity time, right?

TOM
Besides, we have an obligation to our public.

COCO
Not to mention our employees. If I spent all of my time hanging out with the kids, how do you think your salary would get paid, hmmm?

SYLVIE
She has a boyfriend.

TOM
And why didn't you come to us with this information earlier, young lady?

SYLVIE
You don't even know my name!

TOM
That's not the point.

COCO
No, that's not the point.

MRS. BRADY
So tell us about Clover's boyfriend.

SYLVIE
(Shrugs)
He's much older.

TOM
How much older?

SYLVIE
I don't know — maybe 30? 35?

TOM
What the hell are we paying you for?

SYLVIE
You told her she could.

COCO
You expect Mrs. Brady to believe that we told you she could go out with —

TOM
A 35-year old man? Are you crazy?

COCO
That's absurd. I'm going to press criminal charges against you. Negligence.

TOM
Negligence.

SYLVIE
    (near tears)
You did. You told her she could go out with him. He picks her up from school.

COCO
You don't mean —

TOM
No. That can't be.
    (TOM and COCO look at each other)

COCO
Jay picks her up from school.

SYLVIE
That's right.

COCO
(incredulous)
You mean Jay —

TOM
30 -35 my ass! I'm going to kill the bastard!
    (TOM rises and punches his fist in his hand)

COCO
Tom —

MRS. BRADY
    (To SYLVIE)
Who is Jay, dear?

COCO
Our manager.

TOM
    (pacing furiously)
I'm going to kill that cocksucking —

COCO
Tom.
    (indicates MRS. BRADY)
Sit down.

TOM
How long has he been—

COCO
Eighth grade. Since eighth grade.

    (They all sit, silently)

MRS. BRADY
Oh dear.

TOM
Motherfucker.

MRS. BRADY
All the more reason to —

TOM
I'm going to fire him.

COCO
Tom.

TOM
I mean it, CoCo. If I find he's laid one finger on that girl —

SYLVIE
I think he's done more than that.

MRS. BRADY
Again, all the more reason to remove the girl from your care, don't you think?

TOM
I'm gonna fire that sonofa —

COCO
Blackmail.

TOM
Excuse me?

COCO

Blackmail. He doesn't want to lose our business, Tom. We're big properties, even for him.

TOM

Yeah, well, he just blew it. Who told him he could pick her up from school, anyway?

COCO

We did, remember? He offered, and we accepted. It was when we let the, uh, little Mexican nanny go — Graciela. It was right after Graciela.

TOM

I never liked that girl. Jesus. I could kill myself.

COCO

Stop being so dramatic.

TOM

The girl is fifteen.

COCO

We tell Jay that unless he stops seeing Clover, we're dumping him as our manager.

TOM

You don't think we should press charges?

COCO

No.

MRS. BRADY

If I might say something —

                    COCO
Go ahead.

                    MRS. BRADY
This is a critical time in the dissolution of your family. You don't want to do anything that would tarnish the girl's reputation. Or your own.

                    COCO
God. We must look like terrible parents.

                    TOM
We *are* terrible parents, CoCo.

                    MRS. BRADY
A case against your manager could drag on for months. I don't think you want to hold on for that long, do you?

                    TOM
That wasn't the plan.

                    COCO
No.

                    TOM
I still say we fire him.

                    COCO
But then he'll continue to see her anyway.

                    TOM
Not if I kill him first.

                    COCO
Tom —

TOM
That's *my* girl, dammit. She's *my* girl, CoCo.

COCO
She's your daughter.

TOM
She's not my real daughter.

MRS. BRADY
That's an important thing to remember, Tom. She's not your real daughter.

COCO
Isn't Jay still into negotiations with Tim for "Red Moon at Dawn"?

TOM
What's that got to do with anything?

COCO
I thought you wanted that role.

TOM
You think I need Jay to get me "Red Moon at Dawn"? Do you know how much my last film grossed? Do you?

COCO
Tom, your last film was "Cop Killers Three".

TOM
So what are you saying?

COCO
Nothing. It's just — well, you have a reputation as an action figure kind of actor. That's all.

TOM
(Shrugs)
And?

COCO
"Red Moon at Dawn" is an arty kind of film. Moody. It would establish you as a real — artist.

TOM
(Shouts)
I am a real artist!

COCO
I know that, dear. But does Tim?

MRS. BRADY
I think we need to —

TOM
Are you saying that child molester Jay has more clout with Tim than I do? I'm a star. I'm big box office.

COCO
Jay grew up with him.

MRS. BRADY
(Clears throat)
Let's just finish up with —

TOM
I know. I need Jay to get me that role.

COCO
And Jay needs you, Tom. He needs us. He needs us more than we — more than *he* — needs Clover.

TOM
I hate you for saying that.
    (Pause)
But I hear you. I hear you.

MRS. BRADY
Okay. I think we've established the fact that you need Jay in your lives.

COCO
Yes.

TOM
Uh huh.

MRS. BRADY
I think we've also established the fact that Jay's relationship with your daughter is inappropriate, therefore, they should not be in contact with one another. Agreed?

COCO
Agreed.

TOM
Agreed.

MRS. BRADY
Okay. Well, I think it's pretty clear what needs to happen with Clover. Now let's move on to —

TOM
Me.

MRS. BRADY
Excuse me?

TOM
It's my turn, right?

MRS. BRADY
Well, I think in light of the circumstances, it's pretty clear —

TOM
Don't you want to know my point of view?

MRS. BRADY
It's already pretty clear —

TOM
She got to talk!

MRS. BRADY
That's true, but —

TOM
You told me that I would have my turn.

MRS. BRADY
We've gone over so much of this already and I hate to waste your time —

TOM
Your fee is part of my divorce settlement. I don't have to do this.
    (TOM leans back in his chair)
I want my turn.

    (Pause)

MRS. BRADY
Okay. Why don't you tell us what made you want to become a father?

TOM
Great. Great stuff.
    (TOM leans forward, a boyish smile on his face.)
Well, I really didn't want to become a Dad. I have so many unresolved issues with my own Dad, I thought, why burden *my* kids with a Dad? So I decided not to have any.

MRS. BRADY
Uh huh. So what happened?

TOM
Well, CoCo showed me the spread with Maisie, and yeah, the woman looked really hot, big belly and all. So I thought, why deprive CoCo the pleasure of looking so great?

COCO
    (Touched)
You never told me that.

TOM
No. I didn't. Then CoCo decided that you know, all that weight gain for just a few months of looking good wasn't really worth it, and we decided to adopt, which was, if I can be frank, a lot more fun than pregnancy would have been.

MRS. BRADY

And why —

TOM

The Carion Agency was superb. They brought us the prettiest young people. I mean, really. Nice, clean, attractive and pregnant young women with — and believe me, guys aren't my thing — really, they're not — *beautiful* young men. Frankly, it was hard to choose.

MRS. BRADY

I'm sure it was.

TOM

But we chose the best. I said to myself, if our unborn daughter — we knew it was a daughter — turns out to be half as good-looking as these young people, we will be very fortunate indeed. Very fortunate.

MRS. BRADY

And you weren't disappointed.

TOM

Are you kidding me? No.

MRS. BRADY

So being a father has been — good for you?

TOM

Absolutely! Are you kidding me? Absolutely!

MRS. BRADY

Well, then, moving forward —

TOM

Except I don't feel like a father.

MRS. BRADY

Excuse me?
(Pause)
What was that, Tom? You don't feel like a father?

TOM

Well, I mean, I feel like I can *act* like a father. CoCo's right, having these kids, being photographed with them, definitely made me feel more in tune with the *idea* of being a father, you know?

MRS. BRADY

Tell me more.

TOM

It's just — I can picture myself with kids because I have kids. Somehow it makes the whole fatherhood thing seem so real. So immediate. Visceral.

MRS. BRADY

Yes, but —

TOM

I think that's the real reason Tim's considering me for "Red Moon at Dawn", and I don't give a damn what you think, CoCo. He reads the trade mags. He's seen me photographed at Lakers' games with the kids.

MRS. BRADY

Is "Red Moon" —

TOM

It's the story of a man whose son is artistic. He's six. The man is having a hard time reaching him; I assume it's because he's not an artist himself but more of a he-man type.

SYLVIE

He's not artistic.

TOM

That's what I just said, uh, you. Babysitter. He's a he-man type.

SYLVIE

I mean the son. He's not artistic. He's autistic.

TOM

What are you, from New York or something?

COCO

How would you know this, Sylvie? Did Jay talk about this with you? That is so — inappropriate.

SYLVIE

I read the book.

TOM

You read the book.

COCO

How could you have read the book? The film hasn't even been produced yet.

TOM

Autistic?

COCO

Yes. Autistic. It's — um —

TOM

Is that a different nationality? Is the son adopted from a different culture? Because then I would really have a leg up.

SYLVIE

Yeah, he's from Autistica.

TOM

Oh, CoCo, it's a shoe-in. Let's just fire Jay. Come on.

MRS. BRADY

I wouldn't do that.

TOM

Why not? My God, do you see the parallels?

MRS. BRADY

Tom, with all due respect, can we please get back on track?

TOM

One more reason to feel like a father. I can use my experience with an adopted son from a different culture to — I don't want to say further — to enhance my film acting. Enhance. That's a good way to put it.

MRS. BRADY

So do you feel paternal towards Walter?

(Silence)

TOM

No.

MRS. BRADY

Could you repeat that?

TOM

No. I do not *feel* paternal. I can *act* paternal, but I do not actually *feel* paternal.

MRS. BRADY

What do you feel?

TOM

I don't know. I don't get Walter, that's for sure. He's always so polite. So — watchful. Careful. I don't understand what makes him tick.

MRS. BRADY

That's a sign, then.

COCO

He's a good boy.

TOM

I didn't say he wasn't a good boy, CoCo. Why are you always putting words —

COCO

I'm not. He's a good boy. Walter is a good boy.

TOM

Fine. He's a good boy. But I don't get him. Is that fair? I don't get him.

MRS. BRADY

What about your daughter?

TOM

What about my — oh, you mean Clover? I love her. With all my heart. She's my little girl.

MRS. BRADY

So you love your daughter?

TOM

I love my — why do you keep calling her my daughter?

MRS. BRADY

Because she's —

TOM

She can't be my daughter. For one thing, she's too pretty!
    (TOM laughs. Nobody else does)

MRS. BRADY

So you wouldn't describe your feelings towards either child as paternal.

TOM

No.

MRS. BRADY

And you, CoCo? Would you describe your feelings towards either child as maternal?

COCO

No…more like an aunt, or a big sister.

MRS. BRADY

That doesn't really count, does it?

                              COCO
No.

                          MRS. BRADY
Okay. Well. I think it's time to take this to the next step.

                              COCO
That's why we're here.

                          MRS. BRADY
Yes. I just need you both to sign these papers.

                              TOM
What's this?

                              COCO
Tom…

                          MRS. BRADY
These are the papers saying that you will relinquish —

                              TOM
I can't sign anything without my lawyer present.

                              COCO
Tom, we went over this before we came.

                              TOM
If we went over this before we came, then why isn't my lawyer here?

                          MRS. BRADY
Tom, we discussed this at length on the telephone. You know why you're here today.

TOM
Who's going to get my kids?

MRS. BRADY
We have found them a good home with an alternative celebrity family.

COCO
Who? It's not Felicia Hotton, is it? Because if it is, well, I can't. I just can't.

TOM
Why not? What did Felicia ever do to you?

COCO
Oh, please. The woman doesn't have a maternal bone in her body.

MRS. BRADY
Here, let me show you.
    (MRS. BRADY hands a folder to TOM and COCO.
    They glance at it and hand it back)

TOM
What happened to her other life partner? The skinny brunette with the nose ring?

MRS. BRADY
Our sister company found her a more appropriate match. Let's just say she wasn't comfortable with the spotlight.

COCO
I could tell. Who's your sister company?

MRS. BRADY
It's called Making the Switch. I could give you their card —

COCO
(Hastily)
No thank you. Maybe Tom —

TOM
I'm good for now.
(He points to folder)
That one doesn't even look gay.

MRS. BRADY
She might not be. But it's a nice life and a very good career move.

COCO
I thought they already had four kids.

MRS. BRADY
They — did. But there were a few issues with two of them, so they were redistributed. Which is lucky for you.

COCO
Are they — good parents?

MRS. BRADY
We think so. Their children have all of the material advantages that yours do. I think it's also a less, how should we say, *public* household? This particular celebrity is not one for being photographed.

TOM
Well, no kidding.

MRS. BRADY
I'm sorry?

TOM
Look at her! I mean, come on!

COCO
Tom, don't be mean.

TOM
Since when are you Mother Theresa?

COCO
You just never know who might be listening.

MRS. BRADY
I assure you, Tom, CoCo, your children will enjoy all of the material comforts of their former home in this one. And as far as the public goes, it should be a flawless transition.

COCO
You don't think anyone will notice?

MRS. BRADY
Just the children.

COCO
Oh.
    (Pause)

TOM
Well, if it's just the kids — I guess that's not so bad.

COCO
No.

TOM
It's not like whole families are affected.

MRS. BRADY
No. Just the children.

COCO
Well, that seems harmless enough.

TOM
It could be a lot worse.

MRS. BRADY
Yes, it could.

TOM
And really, with the new family, I don't think there'll be an excess of lecherous straight men around, looking to take advantage of a beautiful girl like Clover.

MRS. BRADY
With that particular household, it's doubtful.

TOM
That's probably a good thing.

COCO
When will we get to say goodbye?

TOM
I'd like to —

MRS. BRADY

No.

COCO

Why not? We're their —

MRS. BRADY

No. You're not. Not anymore.

COCO

So —

MRS. BRADY

The transition will be easier for them like this, believe me.

COCO

Can you give them these for us?

MRS. BRADY

(Shakes head)

COCO

I prepared them myself. They're just signed headshots -

MRS. BRADY

No, CoCo. It's for the best.

SYLVIE

Walter will be sad.

COCO

Who are you to say that?

SYLVIE

I'm just saying —

COCO

SHUTUP!
    (Everyone stares)
Just — shutup.

    (Silence)

MRS. BRADY

It's always a little sad, dear, but sadness is something you get used to. Believe me. In a few months' time, Walter will barely be able to tell the difference between this situation and his old one.

COCO

Well I should hope he'd be able to tell the difference!

MRS. BRADY

Really. What's one private school compared to another? One sibling compared to another? One new mommy or daddy compared to another? We've always believed that if the grownups are happy, the kids will be, too.

COCO

    (Moved)
That's what we believe, too.

TOM

A lot of people don't get that.

MRS. BRADY

It's a shame, really, that most people don't have your — sophistication. Now — do you have any other questions before you sign?

SYLVIE
Will the children be needing a new nanny?

MRS. BRADY
A new one, perhaps, but not their old one. Any —

SYLVIE
But I really like them.
    (SYLVIE looks as if she's about to cry)

COCO
Oh please. Spare me the drama. You're not even their *mother*, for chrissakes.

SYLVIE
Neither are you.

MRS. BRADY
Being out of a job is probably making you unduly sentimental. Tell you what, Sylvie — why don't I place a call over to the Carion Group? I'm sure they —

SYLVIE
I don't want to have a baby.

MRS. BRADY
No one's asking you to, dear. But they have other services that you might be interested in exploring.

SYLVIE
Like what?

MRS. BRADY
Well, there are certain celebrities who need a little push when it comes to choosing a partner.

SYLVIE
I'd be like a matchmaker?

MRS. BRADY
No. Oh no. You are a very attractive young woman. I'm sure you'd make the perfect partner for a celebrity that's a little hard to —

SYLVIE
No way.

TOM
(Snorts and shakes head)

COCO
You don't know how lucky you are.

SYLVIE
I know.

MRS. BRADY
Well, the offer's there if you'd like it. Any other questions?

TOM
(clears throat. Nods towards SYLVIE)

MRS. BRADY
I'm getting to that.
(Pushes contract towards TOM and COCO)
So, Tom, CoCo, why don't you sign right here?

                    COCO
Okay,
          (COCO signs)

                    TOM
          (Picks up paper, looks at it sternly, hesitates)

                    COCO
Tom —

                    TOM
Alright, alright —
          (TOM signs)

                    MRS. BRADY
And Sylvie, you sign here, dear.

                    SYLVIE
Why do I have to sign?

                    MRS. BRADY
You're the children's nanny. You have to give up your rights, too.

                    SYLVIE
Does this mean I can't see them?

                    MRS. BRADY
We've already covered this.

                    COCO
Oh for God's sake, just sign it.

SYLVIE

Okay.
    (SYLVIE glances at the piece of paper and puts it down)
You must think I'm really stupid.

COCO

Just sign it.

SYLVIE

I'm not signing this.

TOM

Why not?

SYLVIE

This piece of paper guarantees me a one-time payment of $25,000 and a promise of future placement as a nanny.

TOM

I'm in the wrong business.

MRS. BRADY

That's a very generous settlement, Sylvie.

COCO

Yes, it is.

TOM

CoCo, let me handle this.
    (To SYLVIE)
Everyone can be bought.

SYLVIE

Is that what you think?

TOM

Absolutely.

COCO

Are you kidding me? Grow up!

MRS. BRADY

$25,000 is very generous.

SYLVIE

Is it?

TOM

Yes, it is! How old are you, anyway?

SYLVIE

Nineteen.

TOM

Well, it's high time you learned that $25,000 doesn't come around every day.

COCO

Not when you're nineteen. Except in my case, but I was exceptional. I was a model.

SYLVIE

So what you're saying is that everyone can be bought.

TOM

That's right.

COCO

Everyone.

MRS. BRADY
What's your point, dear?

SYLVIE
My point is, that's good to know. Because I'm sure that someone will be interested in buying these photos that I took on my phone of your family album.

TOM
What?

MRS. BRADY
That was not right, Sylvie.

COCO
Those aren't your property! Why would you do that?

SYLVIE
I wanted something to remember the kids by.

COCO
You little —

TOM
Give me that phone!

(SYLVIE takes the phone and shoves it down the front of her pants. TOM makes a lunge for her)

COCO
(Stands and screams)
Tom!

MRS. BRADY
I wouldn't do that! Now everyone! Just calm down! Just — calm — down. Let's all try and be reasonable.
>(TOM and COCO sit. SYLVIE remains standing. MRS. BRADY motions for her to sit. She does, warily)

Now Sylvie, you're just a child. We're offering you $25,000, which is a large sum of money. You're not going to get anywhere near that from the tabloids. They won't care about these photos.

SYLVIE
I wasn't thinking of the tabloids.

COCO
Who were you thinking about?

SYLVIE
Maybe you'd like these pictures.

TOM
I'd like to —
>(TOM makes a strangling motion with his hands)

COCO
Tom…stop it. Just stop it. Sylvie, why would I want pictures of two kids who, as of two signatures ago, are no longer my responsibility?

SYLVIE
You said it yourself. You said you wanted the pictures of you as a young mom. You said you'd never have that opportunity again.

COCO
I did, didn't I? But…there were some nice stills of me taken with my film kids on the set of "Military Wife".

SYLVIE
That's not the same thing!

COCO
No?

SYLVIE
No!

COCO
Why not?

SYLVIE
They're not your kids!

COCO
Neither are Clover and — Walter. Not anymore.

SYLVIE
But this isn't right! You *know* it isn't right! You have to! I know you do!

TOM
Who are you to judge our lives? Do you know who I am?

SYLVIE
Yes, but —

TOM
I am one of the highest grossing box office stars of the last five years, get it? I am *beyond* criticism. My life is *beyond* reproach.

SYLVIE
(Holds pictures out to COCO, pleadingly)
Take them.

COCO

I told you, I'm not —

SYLVIE

I don't want money for them.

COCO
(Stunned)

What?

SYLVIE

I don't want money for them.

MRS. BRADY

This is most unwise —

SYLVIE

I want you to take them.

COCO

What?

SYLVIE

Take them.

COCO
(Looks helplessly at TOM, who shrugs)

SYLVIE

Take them.

MRS. BRADY

CoCo, as your dedoption agent, I strongly advise you not to do that.

SYLVIE

They're your kids.

COCO

But I just —

SYLVIE

Take them. You should have them.
> (SYLVIE slowly takes the cell phone out from the front of her pants. She extends the phone in her hand to COCO, who slowly extends her own hand to take the phone. Their hands hover. MRS. BRADY stands up, reaches forward and grabs the phone. SYLVIE slumps, defeated)

MRS. BRADY

Most unwise.
> (MRS. BRADY remains standing. She presses a buzzer under her desk)

Tom, CoCo, it's been a pleasure. As I've said before, I'm a huge fan of both your work. Huge.
> (MRS. BRADY takes a business card from her desk and hands it to each of them)

Here's my card — on the back you'll find a complete list of our services. Should either of you ever find yourself requiring some discreet and confidential handling of any, let's say, personal matters, don't hesitate to call me. I should also mention that as 98% of our business is repeat, we have monthly retainers available which, over the long term, are more cost-effective.

> (YOUNG WO/MAN steps into the room)

My assistant will show you out.

YOUNG WO/MAN

Right this way. I have a goody bag for each of you.

COCO
(Looks imploringly at SYLVIE. TOM puts his hand on her back and leads her towards the door)

TOM
(Shaking Mrs. Brady's hand)
Thank you! I feel great. Really well done. CoCo?

COCO
(Somewhat dazed)
Thank you.
(COCO extends her hand to MRS. BRADY, who holds onto it for a few seconds comfortingly)

TOM
(to SYLVIE)
And you? You'll never work in this town again. I'll see to it personally.

SYLVIE
Like I want —

TOM
Watch yourself. You hear me, Daisy? Watch yourself.
(TOM flashes a bright smile to MRS. BRADY and he and COCO exit)

MRS. BRADY
What was that about, young lady?

SYLVIE
What? You mean him?

MRS. BRADY
I mean, this.
>(MRS. BRADY holds up SYLVIE's cellphone. SYLVIE jumps up to grab it. MRS. BRADY holds it just out of reach)

SYLVIE
Give me my phone.

MRS. BRADY
>(Calmly and deliberately deletes all of the photos on the cellphone and hands it back)

There you are. Much better.

SYLVIE
You're a terrible person.
>(SYLVIE starts to cry)

MRS. BRADY
I am not a terrible person, Sylvie. I am a businesswoman, yes, but a businesswoman with compassion. I anticipate trends and benefit from them, but it's all played out in a compassionate and caring way.

SYLVIE
Who benefits from you? You just took two lost kids and gave them to some other screwed up celebrity family.

MRS. BRADY
You're young, dear. Young people recover quickly. Tom and CoCo, despite their sophistication, are in a precarious place, and I have taken care of their situation with a minimum of discomfort and a lot of discretion. Everybody's happy.

SYLVIE

How do you know?

MRS. BRADY

Sylvie, in order for me to be successful at my job, I have to use psychology. Do you know what that is?

SYLVIE

I'm not stupid.

MRS. BRADY

Good. So you could see that as much as Tom and CoCo *wanted* to love their children, their love for themselves was so much greater. You do see that, don't you?

SYLVIE

Kids always love their parents. Their parents can be the biggest fuckups in the world, and their kids will still love them. They're kids. Don't you get it?
(SYLVIE gets up to leave)

MRS. BRADY

You know, Sylvie, I don't think you're really cut out to be a nanny.

SYLVIE

That's not true. I like kids.

MRS. BRADY

Oh, I don't dispute that. I would go so far as to say you love kids. Am I right?

SYLVIE

Maybe.

MRS. BRADY
Yet I wouldn't feel entirely comfortable placing you in another nanny situation.

SYLVIE
Is it because of what *he* said?
> (SYLVIE jerks her hand towards the door)

MRS. BRADY
Oh no, dear. After all, if he doesn't even know your name, he can't really damage your reputation now, can he?
> (MRS. BRADY laughs; SYLVIE joins in. She sits, uneasily)

SYLVIE
So why can't I be a nanny?

MRS. BRADY
You could, but you're such a sensitive soul, I think that when all good nanny situations come to their end, as they always do, you'll be sad. It will be too much for you.

SYLVIE
I think I loved Walter and Chloe more than they did.

MRS. BRADY
Probably. You strike me as a very loving girl. Girl! Listen to me. You're not a girl, you're a woman.

SYLVIE
I think I'm good with kids.

MRS. BRADY
I have a very strong feeling that you are.

SYLVIE

I'm not going to be one of those mothers for the Carion Group, if that's what you're thinking.
(SYLVIE rises to leave)

MRS. BRADY

Goodness gracious, Sylvie, please sit down! No! Of course not! I would never in a million years suggest that you should have a baby and give it to people like Tom and CoCo to raise.

SYLVIE

Good.
(She sits down, warily)

MRS. BRADY
(Pushes a manila folder towards SYLVIE)
Dear, take a look at this. Do you know this celebrity?

SYLVIE
(Opens folder)
Sure I do. Doesn't everyone?

MRS. BRADY

How would you like to have a drink with him say, next Monday night, around 11:00, at the Beverly Hills Hotel?

SYLVIE

I can't afford that!

MRS. BRADY

Sylvie, nobody expects you to pay. The gentleman will pay. Or we can give you pocket money, if it makes you feel more comfortable.

SYLVIE
Why would I want to meet him?

MRS. BRADY
He's a very lonely, very eligible bachelor. I think he'd like to start a family.

SYLVIE
He can't meet girls?

MRS. BRADY
He's very fussy, very picky. So many girls in Hollywood are shallow and self-centered. He needs someone more like you, but Sylvie, women like you are a rare thing here.

SYLVIE
(Stares at picture)
He's old.

MRS. BRADY
He's not that old.

SYLVIE
He's got to be in his forties.

MRS. BRADY
And if you were the kind of person who cared about money, which I know you're not, I would have to be completely honest and tell you that there's a lot of money in it for you. A lot.

SYLVIE
I don't need money.

MRS. BRADY

And, the most important thing, your very own baby. One that nobody can take away from you.

SYLVIE

I'm only nineteen. I'm too young to have a baby.

MRS. BRADY

Oh, Sylvie, you don't want to wait too long. So many actresses in their twenties and thirties are having trouble conceiving.

SYLVIE

But what about — you know, the famous guy's wife, what's her name— she's having a baby, and she's 48!

MRS. BRADY

You are young, aren't you?

SYLVIE

I just read —

MRS. BRADY

Those are donor eggs.

SYLVIE

How do you —

MRS BRADY

A lovely young woman from the Carion Group. I brokered the deal myself.

SYLVIE

Oh.

MRS. BRADY
You don't really want to go that route, do you?

SYLVIE
No!

MRS. BRADY
The Beverly Hills Hotel, Monday night, at 11:00. Will you be there?

SYLVIE
(Takes another long look at photo in folder)
I guess so.

MRS. BRADY
Good. This is a smart move, Sylvie, and one you won't regret. Now, why don't I take you around the corner so that my assistant can get all of your vital information? Then the two of you can go on a shopping spree for some new outfits.

SYLVIE
I can't —

MRS. BRADY
No worries, dear, the outfits are a gift from us.

SYLVIE
You mean I'll get to keep them?

MRS. BRADY
(Escorting SYLVIE from the room as LIGHTS FADE)
Oh, I think so. I have a good feeling we're going to know each other for a very very long time.

END OF PLAY

Whose Bag Is It, Anyway?

Whose Bag Is It, Anyway?
Cast of Characters

MOM: A 45-50 year old woman. She wears a jogging suit.

DAUGHTER: A 17-year old senior in high school. She is dressed for a casual night with friends.

DAD: A 45-50 year old man. He is dressed for an evening in front of the television at home.

Scene

A living room in America.

Time

The present.

Setting: A living room in America. There is a table, with two or three chairs around it, perhaps a couch or a bookcase in the background.

At Rise: It is early evening. MOM and DAD are seated at the table, reading. A bong and a bag of marijuana are in the center of the table.

(DAUGTER enters from offstage)

MOM
Hey, honey. Going out tonight?

DAUGHTER
Yeah.

DAD
Where are you off to?

DAUGHTER
A bunch of us are hanging out at Jen's house.

DAD
Oh. Sounds like fun.

MOM
How are you getting there?

DAUGHTER
Linda's picking me up.

             DAUGHTER, continued
         (notices bong and bag of marijuana)
What's this?

                    MOM
You know what this is.

                    DAD
You can't fool us.

                  DAUGHTER
Where did you find this?

                    MOM
We have our ways.

                    DAD
We're not as "uncool" as you might think.

                  DAUGHTER
Seriously. Where did you get this?

        (MOM and DAD look at DAUGHTER sternly)

                    MOM
Where do you think we'd get it?

                    DAD
Who do you think we'd get it from?

                  DAUGHTER
I have no idea!

MOM

Really.

(MOM and DAD look at each other, then at DAUGHTER. Silence)

DAUGHTER

I'm going to wait outside.

DAD

Not so fast, young lady.

DAUGHTER

What? What did I do?

(MOM nods towards bong and bag)

DAUGHTER

That's not mine!

MOM

Oh.

DAD

Okay.

MOM

So…

DAUGHTER

It's not mine! What do you want me to say? It's not mine!

(MOM and DAD break into grins)

DAD
We know that, honey!

MOM
And I hope you know that we would never go through your things. You know that, right, honey?

DAUGHTER
Yeah.

MOM
I mean, you do know that…

DAUGHTER
Yeah, I know.

DAD
Good.

DAUGHTER
So…what are you doing with that stuff?

DAD
It has a name, you know.

DAUGHTER
You named it?

DAD
No, but it has a proper name.

MOM
It's not just that stuff.

DAD
No. It has a name.

MOM
Right?

DAUGHTER
Uh huh.

MOM
You know what this is, right?

DAUGHTER
Mom, duh. Of course I know what it is.

DAD
How would you know what it is?

DAUGHTER
Because. Everyone know what it is. My God, I'm not a kid.

MOM
Have you tried it?

DAUGHTER
That?

MOM
Yeah.

DAUGHTER
No!

DAD
Really?

DAUGHTER
Really. No.

MOM
Oh, good.
  (She grabs DAD'S hand).

DAD
We're not too late.

DAUGHTER
Too late for what?

  (MOM and DAD beam at DAUGHTER)

DAD
Look. We weren't born yesterday. It's a tough world out there. A world where kids are doing all kinds of unsavory things. Dope. PCP. XTHC. You name it.

MOM
I'm sure you're under a lot of pressure as a teenager to participate in some pretty unhealthy and illegal activities.

DAUGHTER
Not really.

MOM
Honey.
  (She reaches out for DAUGHTER'S hand).

DAUGHTER
What are you getting at?

MOM
Well —

DAD
We want to get you stoned.

DAUGHTER
(in disbelief)
What?

MOM
We would like you to get high. With us.

DAUGHTER
What?

DAD
Just hear us out.

MOM
Look. At some point in the near future, you're gonna be at a party and someone's going to approach you with a jay, or a bong, and you're going to feel compelled by your peers to take a hit.

DAUGHTER
I —

DAD
We'd rather you tried it in the safety of your own home, with people who care about you, and with pot procured from a reliable source.

DAUGHTER
I — I don't believe this.

MOM
What?

DAUGHTER
I don't believe my parents are asking me to get high!

DAD
Better us than some high school burnout who'll try to take advantage of your altered state!

DAUGHTER
I don't want to get high!

MOM
At least this way, you'll see what it feels like to be high so that you can be prepared for the future.

DAUGHTER
What future?

DAD
The future when you'll be partaking socially!

DAUGHTER
But I don't want to get high!

MOM
Oh, you say that now, but…

DAUGHTER
Seriously! I don't want to get high!

DAD
Really?

DAUGHTER
Really!

MOM
But — this is something you're going to have to face at some point, sweetheart. Okay, maybe not in high school, but in college.

DAUGHTER
I don't want to get high!

DAD
Not even a taste?

DAUGHTER
No!

MOM
Oh.

DAD
Huh.
    (MOM and DAD brood)

DAUGHTER
I'm sorry.

MOM
    (Shrugs)
It's okay.

DAD
You know, it's — it's not for — you don't even want to try it?

DAUGHTER
No.
    (Silence)

MOM
I just don't want you to be hurt.

DAUGHTER
How can I be hurt if I'm not going to try it?

MOM
I guess.

DAD
Are you sure?

DAUGHTER
I told you, I don't want to get high.

MOM
Okay.

DAD
It's okay. We heard you the first time.

DAUGHTER
You seem disappointed.

MOM
No. We're not — are we?
    (Looks at DAD)

DAD
No. Who needs to get stoned, anyway?

DAUGHTER
That's not why you did this?

MOM
Did what?

DAUGHTER
This whole bag thing. That's not why you did it, is it? So that you two could get stoned?

DAD
    (Indignant)
No!

MOM
How could you even think that? We could get stoned anytime we want. We just don't want to. Right?
    (Looks at DAD)

DAD
Right.

DAUGHTER
So where did you get it?

MOM
Get what?

DAD
What are you talking about?

DAUGHTER
You know. The dope. Where did you get it?

MOM
Dope? Did you just refer to this as dope?

DAD
Where did you learn that phrase, young lady?

DAUGHTER
Don't turn this on me. Where did you get it?

(MOM and DAD are silent)

Alright. Fine. Do I have to call your friends?

(MOM and DAD look at each other)

MOM
What friends?

DAUGHTER
Oh, I don't know. Maybe the Chauncys? Should I call them?
(Picks up cordless phone)
Maybe they can tell me where you picked this up?

MOM
No!

DAD
Dick Chauncy sits on the Town Planning Board, for chrissakes!

DAUGHTER
I'm just saying, maybe he knows —

DAD
He knows nothing.
>(Takes phone away from DAUGHTER).

DAUGHTER
You're acting awfully upset.

DAD
Just get the Chauncys out of your head, will you?

DAUGHTER
So where did you get the stuff?

>(MOM and DAD sit silently. They look around, uncomfortable)

DAUGHTER
Okay. Be that way. But no one's moving from this table until you tell me where you got it.

MOM
Fine.

DAD
I don't need to be anywhere .

MOM
Nope. I'm not the one going anywhere.

>(Silence)

MOM	DAD
It was —	Someone -

MOM

You go 'head.

DAD

No, you.

MOM

Okay. It was for the Little League team. You know, one of those boys outside of the 7 Eleven with a can and some little bags trying to make money for the Little League team.

DAD

Yeah. Twelve bucks a bag.

MOM

It was very reasonable.

DAD

I'll say.

DAUGHTER

You expect me to believe that a boy was standing outside the 7-Eleven selling weed to raise money for Little League?

MOM

You don't have to believe it —

DAD

But it's true.

DAUGHTER

Okay. Fine. Whatever. Why don't we just flush this bag down the toilet and forget we had this conversation, okay?

MOM
Okay.

DAD
Sure.
    (He gets up to take bag of weed to the bathroom)
Are you sure you don't want to —

DAUGHTER
Positive.

MOM
I just feel badly that you don't trust your Dad and I enough to confide in us.

DAUGHTER
There's nothing to confide!

MOM
Okay. I just want you to know, though, that if there's anything —

DAUGHTER
Anything?

MOM
Absolutely.

DAUGHTER
Well, there is something —

MOM
    (leans in, nods encouragingly)

           DAUGHTER
Have you ever been on the Pill?

             MOM
I'm sorry, honey, I didn't hear you. Are kids pushing pills on you these days?

           DAUGHTER
No, not pills. The Pill. Birth control.

             MOM
Excuse me? What did you say?

           DAUGHTER
Birth control pills.

             MOM
Harold, get in here.

             DAD
     (Runs in from bathroom)
What? What is it?

             MOM
Tell him.

           DAUGHTER
Nothing. Just forget it!

             MOM
Your daughter — our little girl - was asking me about birth control pills!

DAD

She — what?

MOM

You heard me. Don't make me say it again.

DAD

Birth control pills?

DAUGHTER

Forget it! Forget I said anything!

DAD

What do you think this is, some kind of free love clinic?

MOM

Now look what you've done. You've upset your father.

DAUGHTER

You asked me —

DAD

No! We were trying to prepare you for college party life, not an orgy!

MOM

I — I can't even talk about this. Which one of your friends put this idea in your head?

DAUGHTER

Nobody! I'm going to go wait downstairs for Linda.
    (The doorbell rings)
I have to go. That's Linda.

DAD
Be home by 12:00 — no, make that 11:00, you hear me?

MOM
And no more talk of this — this filth! Don't forget, you are a lady!

DAD
And if anyone at this gathering decides to do up some birth control pills, you come home immediately, young lady.

DAUGHTER
Goodbye.
 (She kisses them each on the cheek and leaves)

DAD
Kids.
 (Shakes head)
I don't get it.

MOM
I'm so — disturbed. What is this generation coming to?
 (Silence)

DAD
I saved a little bit of the pot.

 (DAD pulls out the water pipe)

MOM
Fire it up.
 (DAD packs the pipe as LIGHTS FADE.)

END OF PLAY

The Real Family

The Real Family
Cast of Characters

BRIAN: An eighteen year old, nondescript male. He wears a blazer, jeans, and has a small suitcase

DAD: A man in his early to late forties, bespectacled, conservatively dressed

MOM: A woman in her early to late forties, wearing a dress and apron

Scene
DAD and MOM's kitchen, somewhere in suburbia

Time
The present.

Setting: The suburban kitchen of DAD and MOM, which is also the childhood home of BRIAN

At Rise: It is morning. BRIAN, DAD and MOM have finished breakfast and are seated around the kitchen table.

BRIAN
Mom, Dad — I want to thank you for everything you've done for me.

DAD
Brian —

MOM
Oh honey —

BRIAN
But — it's time for me to seek out my real parents.

MOM
    (sobs)
Oh, Brian —

DAD
I wish you wouldn't, son.

BRIAN

Mom, Dad — you guys have been like real parents to me. Believe me when I say that I couldn't have been raised by two nicer people.

MOM

Brian —

BRIAN

But it's time for me to find out who I am. Where I really come from. What the story is behind the people who gave birth to me and then gave me away.

DAD

Don't do this, son.

BRIAN

You said my mother — I mean, my birth mother — was born in New York City, right?

MOM

We did —

BRIAN

And my birth dad — he was some sort of European count passing through on his way to a basketball tournament?

DAD

Well —

BRIAN

And my birth mom was a rising supermodel when she got pregnant?

MOM

Um —

BRIAN
God, it must have been awful. She must have thought it would ruin her career. Did my birth records give her name?
(MOM and DAD look at each other)

DAD
(clears throat)
Not exactly.

BRIAN
That's okay. One thing's always puzzled me, though — if he played basketball and she was a rising supermodel, wouldn't that make me tall? I mean, taller than most people?

(MOM and DAD look at each other uncomfortably)

BRIAN
'Coz I'm not really that tall. I'm more like you guys.

(Silence)

BRIAN
Okay. Well, I guess I'm off to New York City, to locate the birth record.
(BRIAN stands up)

DAD
Son, I can't let you do this.

BRIAN
You can't stop me, Dad.

MOM
Brian, there's something we're not telling you.

BRIAN

What? What is it?
 (sees the looks on their faces)
What? Oh. What, she wasn't a supermodel? Is that it?

DAD

That's part of it.

BRIAN

Part of it? What's the rest? He wasn't European royalty?

MOM

Not exactly.

BRIAN

What? Are you trying to tell me that you lied about my birth parents?

MOM

Mmmmm—

BRIAN

What, were they teenagers or something? Trailer trash people? Criminals? Is my biological father in prison somewhere?
 (BRIAN sits again, stunned)

DAD

God.

BRIAN

You've got to tell me. Please. I can take it.

 (MOM and DAD look helplessly at one another)

DAD
Son, I don't know how to say this.
  (looks at wife)
You do it.

MOM
Thanks a lot.
  (She takes a deep breath)
Brian, uh, all those years when you thought you were — um —

BRIAN
Part of a more exotic and successful family?

MOM
Yeah.

DAD
You weren't.

BRIAN
Oh.
  (They all sit in silence)
So who were my real parents?

MOM
You're looking at them.

DAD
We lied to you, Brian.

MOM
I'm so sorry, Brian.
  (she wipes eyes)

BRIAN
What are you saying?

DAD
You're not adopted.

BRIAN
What?

DAD
You're not adopted. You're actually — our biological son.

MOM
Brian, I'm so sorry. We should have told you —

BRIAN
Are you kidding me? *You're* my biological parents?

DAD
You heard us.

BRIAN
You're my biological parents?

MOM
Brian — we're so sorry.

BRIAN
Wait a minute — what about Tony?

DAD
What about Tony?

BRIAN

He's not — oh, God.

MOM

What?

BRIAN

Don't even tell me Tony's my real brother.

DAD

Of course he's your real brother.

BRIAN

Jesus!

MOM

What? You boys have always gotten along.

BRIAN

Yeah, that's because I didn't think he was my real brother! He's a total geek! I felt badly for him!

MOM

Stop that. He's your brother.

BRIAN

Why didn't you tell me sooner?

DAD

Well, we tried.

MOM

A few times.

BRIAN

Not hard enough!

MOM

I know.

BRIAN

I feel so — awful. And normal.

DAD

Maybe we should have waited to tell him.

MOM

Jonathan, he's 18! When were we going to tell him?

DAD

I'm just saying —

MOM

He was about to go to New York and find his birth family, for Pete's sake.

BRIAN

I was totally looking forward to meeting them. How could you do this?

MOM

We just wanted you to feel better about yourself.

BRIAN

I can't believe you guys are my real parents.

DAD

Believe it, son.

BRIAN
I always wondered why I wasn't tall. Or athletic. Or even good-looking.

MOM
But wasn't it nice thinking that you real mom was a supermodel?

BRIAN
Yeah. Real nice. It was a good story. It made me a lot of friends.

DAD
Sure it did.

BRIAN
Why did you make this up?

MOM
Well —

DAD
It's complicated. You were an insecure kid.

BRIAN
So?

DAD
I don't know, Brian. I think it was during the father/son softball game for church. You had just struck out, and I was up at bat — remember?

BRIAN
No.

MOM
He must have blocked it out.

                              DAD

We had two outs. The other team was ahead by one. It was the last inning.

                             BRIAN

God, now I remember.

                              DAD

I was up at bat. I, uh, was never much of an athlete. More of an intellectual.

                             BRIAN

Uh-huh.

                              DAD

Anyway, I struck out.

                             BRIAN

I remember.

                              DAD

The look on your face — it was awful.

                             BRIAN

Well —

                              DAD

Face it, son, you were ashamed of me.

                             BRIAN

Maybe a little.

DAD
You barely spoke to me on the ride home.

BRIAN
I was — humiliated.

DAD
That's when I told you the story of the Count who played basketball. Your birth father.

BRIAN
That's right. I remember.

DAD
You remember. You perked right up.

BRIAN
Yeah. I'm sorry, Dad.

DAD
That's okay, son.

BRIAN
So why did you have to pretend that my birth mom was a supermodel?

DAD
It made for a good story.

MOM
Didn't you ever wonder why all those years we wouldn't let you tell Tony that you were adopted?

BRIAN
I figured it was because you didn't want him to be jealous.

MOM
Oh.

(Silence)

DAD
Are you okay, son?

BRIAN
I don't know. I guess I feel a little — empty. Like I don't know who I am anymore.

MOM
You're you, honey. You're the same person.

BRIAN
Nah. I'm not — special.

DAD
That's not true!

MOM
Of course you are!

BRIAN
Oh, come on. At least before, between the European royalty star athlete and the supermodel, I had a chance. Now I'm just — me.

DAD
What's wrong with that?

MOM
You're fine just the way you are. You always were.

BRIAN
If I was fine, then why did you lie?

DAD
Because of us, son. We didn't want you to be ashamed of us.

BRIAN
Well, I wasn't.
    (They look at him)
It's true! I wasn't!

MOM
Admit it, Brian. That's because you thought we were just nice strangers who were raising you, right?

BRIAN
Well —

DAD
Come on. You can't fool us. We're your parents.

BRIAN
I guess you're right. I thought you guys were nice strangers. I figured that once I told my birth parents what good folks you were, maybe they'd give you some money.

MOM
You're kidding me!

DAD
That's really thoughtful of you.

BRIAN
Well, I didn't want them to think you two did a bad job.

MOM
I'm touched.

BRIAN
You were good parents.

DAD
Thank you, son.

BRIAN
But — you really are telling me the truth? There's no tall, good-looking, rich birth parents to contact?

DAD
I'm afraid not.

MOM
We're sorry.

BRIAN
So what do I do now?

MOM
Well…why don't you talk to your birth parents? Find out what makes them tick? What you might have in common?

BRIAN
But — you guys are my birth parents.

DAD
So? What do you want to know?

BRIAN
I already know you. You're my — parents.

(Pause)

MOM
Did you know that in seventh grade, your father won a national poetry contest?

BRIAN
No. I didn't know you wrote poems.

DAD
I did. I won a beautiful gold watch, and my poem was published in a magazine.

BRIAN
Really? Can I see it?

DAD
I think I may have it somewhere in the attic.

MOM
We should look. And while we're up there, maybe we'll find my trophy.

BRIAN
You won a trophy?

MOM
Girls' basketball championship, senior year.

BRIAN
You were an athlete?

MOM
Yup.

BRIAN
I'd like to see it.

(MOM, DAD and BRIAN stand)

DAD
While we're up there, remind me to tell you about the time your grandpa caught the biggest fish on Old Silver Beach.......

(as LIGHTS fade)

END OF PLAY

Fomite

A fomite is a medium capable of transmitting infectious organisms from one individual to another.

"The activity of art is based on the capacity of people to be infected by the feelings of others." Tolstoy, *What Is Art?*

Writing a review on Amazon, Good Reads, Shelfari, Library Thing or other social media sites for readers will help the progress of independent publishing. To submit a review, go to the book page on any of the sites and follow the links for reviews. Books from independent presses rely on reader to reader communications.

Visit http://www.fomitepress.com/FOMITE/Our_Books.html for more information or to order any of our books.

As It Is On Earth
Peter M Wheelwright

Dons of Time
Greg Guma

Loisaida
Dan Chodorkoff

My Father's Keeper
Andrew Potok

My God, What Have We Done
Susan V Weiss

Rafi's World
Fred Russell

Fomite

The Co-Conspirator's Tale
Ron Jacobs

Short Order Frame Up
Ron Jacobs

All the Sinners Saints
Ron Jacobs

Travers' Inferno
L. E. Smith

The Consequence of Gesture
L. E. Smith

Raven or Crow
Joshua Amses

Sinfonia Bulgarica
Zdravka Evtimova

The Good Muslim
of Jackson Heights
Jaysinh Birjépatil

The Moment Before an Injury
Joshua Amses

Fomite

The Return of
Jason Green
Suzi Wizowaty

Victor Rand
David Brizeri

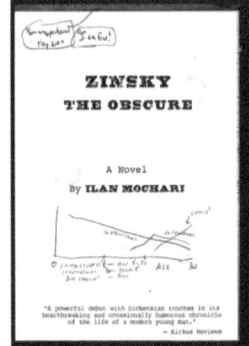

Zinsky the Obscure
Ilan Mochari

Body of Work
Andrei Guruianu

Carts and Other Stories
Zdravka Evtimova

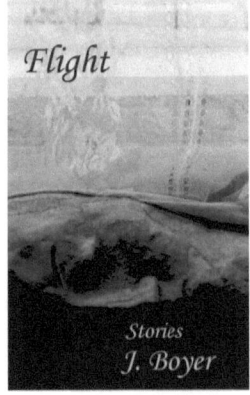

Flight
Jay Boyer

Love's Labours
Jack Pulaski

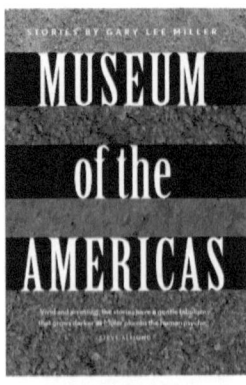

Museum of the Americas
Gary Lee Miller

Saturday Night at Magellan's
Charles Rafferty

Fomite

Signed Confessions
Tom Walker

Still Time
Michael Cocchiarale

Suite for Three Voices
Derek Furr

Unfinished Stories of Girls
Catherine Zobal Dent

Views Cost Extra
L. E. Smith

Visiting Hours
Jennifer Anne Moses

When You Remeber
Deir Yassin
R. L. Green

Alfabestiaro
Antonello Borra

Cycling in Plato's Cave
David Cavanagh

Fomite

AlphaBetaBestiario
Antonello Borra

Entanglements
Tony Magistrale

Everyone Lives Here
Sharon Webster

Four-Way Stop
Sherry Olson

Improvisational Arguments
Anna Faktorovitch

Loosestrife
Greg Delanty

Meanwell
Janice Miller Potter

Roadworthy Creature
Roadworth Craft
Kate Magill

The Derivation of
Cowboys & Indians
Joseph D. Reich

Fomite

The Housing Market
Joseph D. Reich

The Empty Notebook
Interrogates Itself
Susan Thomas

The Hundred Yard
Dash Man
Barry Goldensohn

The Listener Aspires
to the Condition of Music
Barry Goldensohn

The Way None
of This Happened
Mike Breiner

Screwed
Stephen Goldberg

Planet Kasper
Peter Schumann

My Murder
and Other Local News
David Schein

Picking Up the Bodies
James F. Connolly

Fomite

The Falkland Quartet
Tony Whedon

Drawing on Life
Mason Drukman

Among Angelic Orders
Susan Thoma

Confessions of a Carnivore
Diane Lefer

Principles of Navigation
Lynn Sloan

Derail Thie Train Wreck
Daniel Forbes

Free Fall/Caída libre
Tina Escaja

A Guide
to the Western Slopes
Roger Lebovitz

Planet Kasper
Volume Two
Peter Schumann

Fomite

Nothing Beside Remains
Jaysinh Birjépatil

Foreign Tales of
Exemplum and Woe
J. C. Ellefson

Where There Are Two
or More
Elizabeth Genovise

The Inconveniece
of the Wings
Silas Dent Zobal

www.ingramcontent.com/pod-product-compliance
Lightning Source LLC
Chambersburg PA
CBHW021432080526
44588CB00009B/510